QUEEN VICTORIA
AND HER MINISTERS

T. Lawrence pinx. *McInnes sc.*

WILLIAM LAMB, 2ND VISCOUNT MELBOURNE

[*Frontispiece*

32 pp.

QUEEN VICTORIA AND HER MINISTERS

BY

SIR JOHN A. R. MARRIOTT

HONORARY FELLOW (FORMERLY FELLOW AND LECTURER) OF
WORCESTER COLLEGE, OXFORD; LATE M.P. FOR YORK

ILLUSTRATED

NEW YORK
E. P. DUTTON & CO., INC.

QUEEN VICTORIA AND HER MINISTERS

FIRST EDITION

CONTENTS

LIST OF ILLUSTRATIONS

* *By kind permission of the Proprietors of "Punch."*

PREFACE

MUCH has been written, and by many competent pens, about Queen Victoria and the period with which her name will ever be associated. The appearance of yet another book, however modest its purpose and limited its scope, seems, therefore, to demand a word of justification.

It seems probable that, except for the concluding volumes of the biographies of Lord Salisbury and Mr. Chamberlain, we now possess all the original materials which are essential to a study of the period. Those materials, with Martin's *Life of the Prince Consort* (5 vols.) and the nine volumes of the *Letters of Queen Victoria* at the head of the catalogue, are almost overwhelming in their amplitude. But it is only in the last year or two that they have become, in their entirety, available.

Furthermore, there exists, so far as I am aware, no book which attempts to survey the history of the period from the angle here selected.

It is generally agreed that the working of that peculiar form of government known as Constitutional Monarchy was never exhibited to such advantage as during the reign of Queen Victoria, and particularly in the period between 1832 and 1867. That type of constitution presupposes for its success certain qualities both among rulers and ruled, on the possession of which we English people are wont, justifiably or not, to pride ourselves. The outstanding quality is love of compromise. Without a readiness to compromise, without constant give and take, without mutual tolerance, and abundant good-humour, a form of government, combining elements so apparently incongruous as Hereditary Monarchy and Parliamentary Democracy, would evidently be doomed to speedy disaster.

Many countries, attributing to her constitution the astounding prosperity and success of Great Britain in the nineteenth century, have flattered her by attempted imitation. But constitutions are not suitable articles for export. The imitations have generally proved failures.

This little book is in no sense a formal treatise on Constitutional Monarchy. It seeks rather to illustrate, by a conspicuous concrete example, the working of that system in the country of origin. The Letters of Queen Victoria and the Biographies and Memoirs of the ministers of her reign afford ample material for such an illustrative study. On them this book is almost entirely based, and to the editors, authors and publishers of those works I acknowledge my deep obligation.

I am greatly indebted also to Messrs. Bradbury, Agnew & Co., Ltd., the proprietors of *Punch*, for permission to reproduce some of the incomparable cartoons which have appeared in that unique publication. I have often said, and now repeat, that if I had to select any *one* original authority for the history of this period, I should unhesitatingly choose *Punch*. But no such dilemma has been presented to me, and I can, therefore, claim for my little book that it is the work of one who for thirty years or more has been saturating his mind with the political literature of the period.

I must not omit a word of grateful thanks to Mr. G. E. Buckle, author of the later volumes of Disraeli's *Life*, and editor of six volumes of the *Letters of Queen Victoria*, for help on one rather difficult portion of my task. I ought perhaps to add that I have occasionally reproduced a few sentences from some of my own books previously published, and have made a more extensive use of articles contributed by me to the *Quarterly*, *Edinburgh* and *Fortnightly* Reviews. In no case, however, has an article been in these pages textually reproduced.

I have almost entirely avoided footnotes, so tiresome to the ordinary reader, and inappropriate in a book of this kind. But in order to acknowledge my indebtedness, to indicate the main sources of my information, and to help such readers as may desire it to more intensive study of the subject, I print in an appendix a short list of books bearing upon it. The list is, however, a short one and must not be regarded as a formal "bibliography."

J. A. R. MARRIOTT.

CHAPTER I

PROLOGUE—THE VICTORIAN ERA

THE Victorian era is rapidly passing into history. Of the statesmen who held high office in the nineteenth century none now (1933) survive; to the vast majority of the subjects of King George V, Queen Victoria is as much an historical personage as Queen Anne. Between the years 1901 and 1933 there has intervened something more than an ordinary generation. Quite apart from the chasm created by the Great War, deep as that is, we are separated by much more than a mere span of years from the men and women who trod the boards in the Victorian drama. The children who are growing up to-day have come into a world where speed is worshipped as a deity, where the internal combustion engine has transformed not merely the art of war but the daily life of the peaceful citizen, where the gramophone enables us to speak to generations yet unborn; where, thanks to the radio, many millions of King George's subjects can listen, one by his fireside in England, and others it maybe in their isolated homesteads on the Canadian prairie, on the African veldt, or in the Australian bush, to the King's Christmas message as it falls from his own lips.

We are, then, removed, if in time only by decades, by centuries in thought and circumstance, from those who lived their lives in Queen Victoria's reign.

Yet that reign marked an epoch sharply distinguished from the years that preceded it, and in itself of outstanding importance. Dean Inge has expressed the opinion that "the Elizabethan and the Victorian ages will appear to the historian of the future as the twin peaks in which English civilization culminated." Whether that be so or not, even if there be in store for the British race in British lands a future destined to dim the splendours of the past, the Victorian era will still stand out as one of high significance in the history of the British peoples.

This book is concerned with a single and special aspect of the reign—the relations between a Sovereign, strictly conforming to the unwritten law of a Constitutional Monarchy, and her confidential servants. But it may be well to take a brief preliminary survey of the period as a whole.

The reign of Queen Victoria was pre-eminently an era of reform: political, social, fiscal, ecclesiastical and educational; while in the domain of science and in the sphere of Imperial relationships it witnessed nothing less than a revolution. It is sometimes summarily labelled as the age of "Democracy and Empire." The label is apt, and, as far as it goes, accurate. The reign witnessed the transference of supreme political power from the few to the many, from a territorial aristocracy to the great mass of adult citizens, among whom the greater number lived by the labour of their hands. The Parliamentary Reform Acts of 1832, of 1918 and 1928, were indeed outside the limits of the reign, but it was under Queen Victoria that the transition from Aristocracy to Democracy actually took place. Yet an analysis of the Victorian Cabinets makes it clear that executive control continued to rest, for the most part, in the hands of the class that ever since 1714 had ruled England with conspicuous success. A Peel and a Gladstone announced the advent, politically and socially, of the new commercial aristocracy; a Chamberlain, though never actually Prime Minister, brought into the highest sphere of Imperial politics the genius, not of Eton or Harrow, of Oxford or Cambridge, but of a provincial municipality. Out of the ten Victorian Prime Ministers, seven were drawn from the ruling families, and of the remaining three two belonged to a class which by wealth and education was soon to be merged into the aristocracy of birth.

But if the Executive still remained oligarchical, the Legislature soon demonstrated by its output that it felt itself to be answerable to an electorate reinforced by nearly half a million new voters in 1832, by one million in 1867, and by two millions in 1884–5. Until Disraeli "shot Niagara" in 1867 the middle classes were, however, supreme in the electorate, and began increasingly to permeate the House of Commons. Yet the dethronement of the land-owners was due less to the political revolution of 1832 than to the fiscal reforms carried out between 1841 and 1846. The repeal of the Corn Laws marked, as we shall see, the dividing line between the ascendancy of land and that of Industry and Trade. England, which had for centuries been a sheep-walk, which had then given itself up to the plough, became finally a land of towns, factories, mines and shipbuilding yards.

Queen Victoria witnessed, perhaps, the meridian of England's supremacy in commerce and industry. And she herself was entirely sympathetic with the class destined to attain to political supremacy during her reign. It was indeed supremely fortunate, as Mr. Arthur Benson pointed out in his Introduction to the first volume of the Queen's *Letters*, that by a happy intuition the Queen thoroughly understood and could interpret the middle-class point of view. She shared their outstanding characteristics: their common sense, their moderation in all things, their mistrust of enthusiasm and avoidance of extremes, and not least their domestic virtues; equally, she sympathized with their limitations, and was not herself free from some of the prejudices to which they adhered.

This was providential not less for the Sovereign than for her subjects. For when Queen Victoria ascended the throne the general atmosphere of Europe was none too favourable to monarchy. Kingship was on its trial. The first French Revolution had given the monarchical principle, not only in France, a rude shock; and in the first decade of the nineteenth century more than half the Sovereigns in Europe were in exile. The restorations of 1814–15 had given monarchy another chance, but it was still uncertain whether the opportunity would be redeemed. The Legitimist monarchy in France had, in 1830, for the third time been superseded, and had given way to the citizen-kingship of Louis Philippe. The orgy of reaction into which, in Spain and Southern Italy, the Bourbons had plunged, was not likely to commend "Legitimacy" as a principle to people to whom the French Revolution had proclaimed the idea of Liberty, and to whom Napoleon had brought, if not Liberty, at least Equality. In the Federated States of Germany the liberal professions of 1815 had been very imperfectly realized; the Poles had learnt the value of the promises of an Autocrat; the Greeks had lately delivered a successful assault upon the Ottoman Sultanate at Constantinople.

In England the position of the monarchy was, if not critical, none too stable. "Since the century began there had been three kings . . . of whom the first was long an imbecile, the second won the reputation of a profligate, and the third was regarded as little better than a buffoon." Sir Sidney Lee's words may savour somewhat of exaggeration, but it is undeniably true that under George IV the Throne was definitely unpopular, and that under William IV it was, if more popular, even less respected.

> Oh that the free would stamp the impious name
> Of King into the dust.

That was a sentiment more commonly expressed on the Continent than in England; but even in England everything seemed in 1837 to depend on the personality, the character, and wisdom of the Princess who was to ascend the throne which her uncles had done so little to adorn.

Superbly did Queen Victoria redeem the opportunity. She was greatly helped by a concurrence of political opinion. Parliamentary reform was promoted by both the great parties in the State. If the Tories were responsible for giving the parliamentary franchise to the town artisans in 1867, and for democratizing county government in 1888, the Liberals gave the vote to the agricultural labourers in 1884–5, and completed the structure of representative local government by the District and Parish Councils Act of 1894. But if the primary responsibility rests upon Party chiefs, we now know how much credit for making the path smooth for them belongs to her

> Who knew the Season when to take
> Occasion by the hand and make
> The bounds of freedom wider yet,
> By shaping some august decree,
> Which kept her throne unshaken still
> Broad based upon the people's will.

But these words were written in retrospect. The poet could look back upon achievement; the young Queen and her ministers had to look forward.

The prospect was none too promising. In 1837 many wise men thought that England was on the eve of a social revolution. Statesmen and economists, prophets and philanthropists, were anxiously pondering the "condition of

England" question. The condition of England was unquestionably grave; not perhaps quite so grave as Carlyle and Charles Kingsley and other like-minded men supposed; but still grave enough. The times were out of joint; the old social and economic order was dissolved—the order by which man had been bound to man and class to class; the new order had not had time to evolve out of the chaos which had followed the dissolution of the old. The prevailing discontent issued in the movement known as Chartism. Chartism was a complex phenomenon due to a number of convergent causes. Though the demands of the Chartists were mainly political, though it was manhood suffrage, annual parliaments, vote by ballot, payment of members and such things that they asked for, we can see now that the root of the mischief was less political than social and economic. True, there was bitter discontent, due largely to the disappointing (though probably wise) moderation of the Reform Act of 1832. The working classes believed that they had been duped. They showed it later on by their attitude towards the Free Trade movement, which they derided as a middle-class manœuvre. "If you give up your agitation for the Charter to help the Free Traders," said Thomas Cooper, "they will not help you to get the Charter. Don't be deceived by the middle classes again. You helped them to get their votes. You swelled their cry of 'the Bill, the whole Bill, and nothing but the Bill,' but where are the fine promises they made you? Gone to the winds! and now they want to get the Corn Laws repealed, not for your benefit, but for their own. Cheap bread they cry, but they mean low wages. Do not listen to their cant and humbug. Stick to your Charter, you are veritable slaves without your votes." Yet, little as they knew it, dear food had more to do with Chartism than an exclusive suffrage.

The root of the matter was, in fact, economic. The changes of the last half-century had revolutionized the conditions of English industry, and had transformed the face of English social life. The rapid series of mechanical inventions culminating in the application of steam to manufactures; the increased specialization of industry; its concentration in great cities; the growth of the factory system; the expansion of foreign trade; the revolution in agriculture; the rapid extension of enclosures; the growth of large holdings; the extinction of a once prosperous yeomanry; the development of means of communication; Macadam and Brindley, Telford and Watt—these things, these men, had revolutionized the industrial life of England.

The working classes, alike industrial and agricultural, compelled for the first time to rely entirely for their livelihood on weekly wages, were amazed and startled by the rapidity of the changes, and were deeply disappointed in the results accruing to themselves. Wealth, as they saw, was growing by leaps and bounds, but wages rose slowly, prices were exorbitantly high, and employment was far more inconstant than in the former days. There was wealth in abundance, wealth created as they thought mainly by themselves, and yet many of them were starving. They could not understand it; they were bewildered and perplexed. So was Carlyle: "In the midst of plethoric plenty the people perish."

We have had to face hard times ourselves; we have had periods of deep industrial depression, cycles of commercial gloom. But it is doubtful whether we have ever gone through a period so bad as that between the Queen's accession and the great remedial measures of Sir Robert Peel. We can hardly realize now what the facts recorded for us in Blue Books imply.

But we need not go to Blue Books. Mrs. Gaskell has

painted a picture of the Chartist days in lurid but unexaggerated colours in *Mary Barton*; so has Kingsley; so has Carlyle; so has Disraeli in *Sybil*. The sub-title of the latter is terribly significant—the "Two Nations." Into two nations England, said Disraeli, is literally divided—"Two nations between whom there is no intercourse and no sympathy; who are as ignorant of each others' habits, thoughts and feelings as if they were dwellers in different zones or inhabitants of different planets; who are formed by a different breeding, are fed by a different food, are ordered by different manners, and are not governed by the same laws." That was the real *crux* of the problem—the gulf between class and class.

Many remedies were proposed: Carlyle's Neo-industrial-feudalism; the Chartist's Political programme; the remedy actually adopted was that prescribed by Sir Robert Peel. Peel's fiscal reforms knocked the bottom out of the Chartist agitation, though, in fact, the political reforms for which the Chartists then pressed have all, with one unimportant exception, been conceded. But these matters must engage our attention later on. For the moment only the phenomenon itself concerns us, and the phenomenon was, in the early days of the Queen's reign, sufficiently alarming.

The situation was gradually ameliorated not only by the fiscal reforms of Peel, but by a great body of legislative enactments which immensely improved the conditions of work in factories and mines; gave greater security to the savings made by the wage-earners through their benefit societies; facilitated the provision of public parks, baths, and better houses for the town workers; legalized the association of wage-earners in trade unions and protected their funds; made employers responsible for accidents to their workmen; protected the interests of agricultural tenants and merchant seamen; facilitated the sale of settled land and the provision of small holdings and allotments; promoted public health, and in many other ways enlisted the strong arm of the State and the purse of the taxpayer in the beneficent task of improving the condition of the community at large, and in particular of its poorer sections. That the new social and economic conditions brought about by the Industrial Revolution necessitated the intervention of the State cannot be questioned: whether having once abandoned the principles of *laissez-faire* the State was not tempted to go too far in the opposite direction is a controversial question, not appropriate for discussion in these pages.

To one great series of reforms brief reference must, however, be made.

In 1837 the State devoted £20,000 a year to education: and that meagre subvention dated only from 1833. Down to that year the work of educating the children of the poor in England had devolved wholly upon the Churches. The Church of England had done its work through the National Society, founded in 1811 by Andrew Bell; the British and Foreign School Society, founded by Joseph Lancaster and largely maintained by Nonconformists, had been in operation three years longer. After the passing of the Reform Bill of 1832, the State decided that it must take a hand in the education of its citizens, but its assistance was given through the societies named. The subventions were gradually increased; the principle of "payment by results" was introduced in 1861, and in 1870 Mr. Forster's great Act was passed to provide elementary schools in every district where the provision made by voluntary effort and by the Churches was inadequate. But the main reliance continued to be on voluntary efforts assisted by subventions from taxes and rates. A great change was, however, effected by Acts passed in 1876 and

1880, when elementary education was made compulsory, and by that of 1891 which made it gratuitous.

Meanwhile, the State was beginning to concern itself not only with elementary, but with secondary, technical and university education. The *Endowed Schools Act of 1869* made large sums derived from charitable trusts available for secondary education, though it was not until the passing of the *Technical Instruction Act* (1889) that any effective step was taken towards evolving a coherent system of secondary education for the nation at large. The still more important Act passed in 1902 lies just outside the Queen's reign.

Nor did the ancient Universities escape the attention of a reformed Parliament. Down to 1832 university education in England was provided only by Oxford and Cambridge; and even there for none except members of the Church of England. At Cambridge Nonconformists were indeed permitted to reside and enter for examinations, but they could not proceed to a degree. At Oxford not only graduation but matriculation was subject to a religious test. After the legislation of 1825 and 1829, which repealed the Test Acts and admitted Roman Catholics and Protestant Nonconformists to the full rights of citizenship, still more after the Act of 1832, which brought them in increasing numbers into the Legislature, the anomaly and injustice of university tests was increasingly realized. Royal Commissions were appointed for Oxford and Cambridge in 1850, and many reforms, both domestic and external, followed upon the publication of their Reports. By a series of Acts passed between 1854 and 1871, all religious tests were, with some few and reasonable exceptions, abolished both at Oxford and Cambridge; drastic domestic reforms were also carried through, and thus the two ancient Universities became, in the widest sense of the term, truly national institutions, not only opening their own doors wide to all classes and creeds, but by means of local lectures and local examinations diffusing their influence throughout the land.

The local or "extension" lectures given by Oxford and Cambridge graduates were largely responsible for the multiplication of local universities and university colleges. A third University had been established at Durham in 1832, and four years later London University came into being, but only as an examining body, until in 1900 it was endowed with the full status of a teaching University with a number of constituent colleges. Owens College, Manchester, the germ of a future University, was established in 1851; Mason's College, Birmingham (also destined to expand into a University), in 1875; while between 1876 and 1926 University Colleges (in most cases with similar destiny) were established at Bristol, Liverpool, Sheffield, Nottingham, Reading and Exeter. Thus tardily, but effectively, did Victorian England follow the advice of Robert Lowe, and, having conferred political power upon the mass of her citizens, proceed to educate them in the duties of citizenship.

Closely connected with the widening and deepening of the channels of national education was the progress made during this wonderful era in scientific discovery and invention. This is not the place, nor is mine the pen, to estimate the achievements registered in this sphere. But every layman is aware that, thanks to these inventions and discoveries, the barriers of space and time have been to a large extent annihilated; that human suffering has been relieved; much human waste been prevented, and that the whole art of living has been entirely transformed. Mr. (afterwards the Earl of) Balfour, surveying from the standpoint of 1900 the history of the nineteenth century, found its characteristic note in the growth of scientific knowledge, and more particularly in its application to industry. "The most important and the most fundamental differences which separate the present from preceding ages," are . . . "to be found in the cumulative products of scientific research, to which no other period offers a precedent or a parallel. No single discovery, it may be, can be compared in its results to that of Copernicus. No single discoverer can be compared in genius to Newton. But in their total effects the advances made by the nineteenth century are not to be matched. . . . But not only is this surprising increase of knowledge new, but the use to which it has been put is new also. . . . Speaking broadly, it was not till the present century that the laboratory and the workshop were brought into intimate connection: that the man of practice began humbly to wait on the man of theory; that the man of practice even discovered that a little theory would do him no irretrievable damage in the prosecution of his business."

Detailed illustration of the truth of Lord Balfour's observation must be sought, and can easily be found, elsewhere. There is, however, one aspect of scientific discovery which is of cardinal importance in relation to politics. Thanks to the revolution effected by science in the means of transport and communication, the globe has shrunk, the whole world has become a political and geographical unit. "The result is," as General Smuts has suggestively said, "that problems which a century ago, or even fifty years ago, were exclusively European, now concern the whole world." In fine, the era of *welt-politik* has arrived.

This shortening of distances, this shrinkage of the globe, has had immensely important repercussions alike in the sphere of industry and of politics. Inevitably it has encouraged the competition among the highly industrialized nations of Europe for possession of tropical dependencies. The large-scale production of commodities facilitated by mechanical inventions and the accumulation of capital has led to a scramble on the one hand for the raw materials without a large supply of which modern productive processes are impotent, and on the other for markets in which to dispose of the surplus commodities produced by those processes in such profusion. Many of the raw materials essential to modern industry—vegetable and mineral oils, cotton, sisal, rubber, jute, etc.—can be obtained only from the tropics. Hence, as General Smuts observed, the anxiety displayed by the industrialized countries of Europe for a place in the tropical sun.

This anxiety to command a supply of raw materials, and to find protected markets for the disposal of manufactured products, led, in the latter part of the Victorian era, to a revival of the old idea of "plantations"—oversea estates to be walled for the benefit of the home-proprietors. Such "plantations," characteristic of the old colonial system, were denounced in the eighteenth century by Adam Smith as unworthy of any nation, except a nation of shopkeepers, and not really desirable even for them.

The secession of the English colonies in America added practical emphasis to the theoretic teaching of Adam Smith, and established, it was thought, the accuracy of Turgot's prognosis: "Colonies were little fruits which would cling to the tree only until they ripened."

Yet, notwithstanding the warnings of philosophers, Great Britain utilized a recent discovery of Captain Cook's to establish a colony (1788) at Botany Bay in Australia—albeit only for the reception of convicts, naturally rejected, after 1783, by the Carolinas. Another result of the secession of the United States, combined with the stubborn patriotism of the United Empire Loyalists, was the beginning of systematic colonization in Canada—hitherto almost exclusively French. At the Peace of 1814 we retained

Ceylon and Cape Colony captured from the Dutch during the Napoleonic wars. But the motive was primarily strategical, and not until some years later did British colonists begin to establish themselves in South Africa.

It is, therefore, hardly an exaggeration to say that when Queen Victoria came to the throne England had lost her first Colonial Empire, and had made little progress with the establishment of the second. British India was still under the rule of the East India Company, though since 1782 the Company had, in fact, shared sovereignty with the Board of Control; in area it was still far short of the India of to-day, while its gross revenue amounted to no more than £22,000,000, as compared with nearly £220,000,000 (Central and Provincial) to-day. Excluding India the population of the colonies and dependencies amounted in 1837 to less than 4,000,000, to which British North America contributed 1,250,000.

Nor were the Government or the people greatly concerned about the overseas Empire as a whole. The West Indies were a source of profit to a limited class; but apart from them the Empire was little regarded. In 1837 both Canadas (English and French) were in open rebellion. The rebellion was promptly suppressed, and with the mission and report of Lord Durham, Canada entered on a new and important period of its history. But during the first half of the Queen's reign the Manchester School dominated English policy; the doctrine of *laissez-faire* was consistently held and applied by the Colonial Office (not until 1854 separated from the War Office) as by other Departments of State. It was assumed that these Colonies, which were already advancing by gradual stages towards self-government, would in time follow the example of the United States and declare their independence; and few responsible politicians cared how soon that time arrived. It was, indeed, the accepted policy of the Colonial Office to hasten it. "To ripen these communities to the earliest possible maturity, social, political, commercial, to qualify them by all the appliances within the reach of the parent State for present self-government and eventual independence is now the universally admitted aim of our colonial policy." So Mr. Arthur Mills wrote in 1856, and his words represented no more and no less than the naked truth. Cobden put the same point, more crudely and more brutally, but not less accurately, when he said: "The Colonial system . . . can never be got rid of except by the indirect process of Free Trade, which will gradually and imperceptibly loosen the bands which unite our Colonies to us by a mistaken notion of self-interest." [1] These views were widely held.

Nowhere did the latter years of the reign present a more splendid and dazzling contrast to the earlier than in the sphere of Imperial relations: and to no sphere of government did the monarchy make so direct and important a contribution. The Crown began to stand out more and more conspicuously as the symbol of Imperial unity. The loyalty of the oversea dominions is evoked not by an institution but by a person, not by a Parliament which has forfeited and indeed surrendered even the formal title of Imperial, but by a King-Emperor.

Apart from Imperial affairs, did the Crown lose ground during the Victorian era? The answer to that question must not be anticipated, since it is the main purpose of this book to supply it. Meanwhile, two or three preliminary observations seem pertinent. The *formal* powers of the Crown remained intact. The formal prerogatives and powers of Queen Victoria were virtually identical with

[1] Morley: *Cobden*, I, 230.

those of Queen Elizabeth. Parliament still consists of King (or Queen), Lords and Commons. The Crown is still the executive ruler of the Kingdom. Members of the Cabinet are still his or her "servants." The Crown is still the sole source of justice and the fountain of honour. Some seventy years ago Walter Bagehot startled his contemporaries by telling them what "the retired widow at Windsor" could do without consulting Parliament, and King George habitually exercises powers never contemplated by Queen Victoria. But this refers to *formal* powers now in fact exercised by ministers and departments. The actual powers of the Crown are a different matter. With admirable perspicuity Bagehot analysed them; and, except in regard to Imperial affairs (which he characteristically ignored), his analysis could to-day hardly be improved upon. The monarchy supplies an intelligible figure-head to the State; it "consecrates our whole State"; it is the head of Society; the head of our *morality*; it acts as a *disguise* to the crudities of party government. But apart from this the Crown retained three *real* political functions of immense though varying importance: the right to be consulted and therefore to advise; the right to encourage, and the right to warn. "We shall never know," he added, "but when history is written our children may know what we owe to the Queen and Prince Albert."

More than two generations have passed since those words were written; we now study the Victorian era as "History"; we have been admitted to the arcana of State; the motives which inspired the policy of the leading actors in the drama have been to a large extent revealed. We can, therefore, appreciate the debt which we owe to Queen Victoria on the one hand and to her confidential advisers on the other.

To help towards a wider if not a deeper appreciation is the main purpose of the pages that follow.

what is the crown?

CHAPTER II

LORD MELBOURNE—THE EDUCATION OF A QUEEN

THE Queen's first Prime Minister was William Lamb, second Viscount Melbourne.[1] Melbourne's paternity was doubtful, but whether he was the son of the first Viscount, or, as gossip said, of the Earl of Egremont, he was undoubtedly the son of his mother. She was Elizabeth, the only daughter of Sir Ralph Milbanke, fifth baronet of Halnaby in the County of York. Inheriting from his father an ample fortune and a peerage, and brains from his mother; endowed with a handsome presence, a beautiful voice, and a perfect temper, Melbourne was evidently destined to play a distinguished part in public affairs. He played it with eminent success, and performed a service to his country which can only be described as unique. To him, more than to any other individual, Queen Victoria owed that thorough grounding in the difficult art of Constitutional Monarchy which contributed to make her the great Sovereign she became. Yet in the treatment of Melbourne himself Fate has been more than ordinarily capricious. To his contemporaries he was in every sense of the word a great figure. But their admiration was not based on discernment. Extreme sensitiveness led him to

[1] B. 1779; ed. Eton and Trinity College, Cambridge; m. (1805) Lady Caroline Ponsonby, d. of 3rd E. of Bessborough; M.P. Leominster (Whig), 1806; Irish Secretary under Canning and Wellington, 1827--8; s. father 1829; Home Secretary under Grey (1830-4); P.M. (1834) and 1835-41; d. 1848.

wear a mask. Immensely industrious and of serious purpose, he posed as an indolent dilettante; his great learning he bore so lightly that few suspected its existence; so greatly did he detest exaggeration that men thought him cold; his antipathy to hypocrisy made him seem cynical; devoid of vanity, he was still conscious of great powers, and, though seemingly indifferent to honours and place, he was in fact exceedingly ambitious. Sydney Smith was shrewd enough to penetrate the disguise he habitually assumed: "Our Viscount," he wrote, "is somewhat of an impostor . . . I am sorry to hurt any man's feelings and to brush away the magnificent fabric of levity and gaiety he has reared, but I accuse our minister of honesty and diligence." Like recognized like.

To his personal charm no one could be insensible. "His laugh," wrote the late Lord Esher, "was frequent and the most joyous possible, his voice so deep and musical that to hear him say the most ordinary thing was a pleasure; and his frankness, his freedom from affectation and his peculiar humour rendered almost everything he said, however easy and natural, quite original."

Melbourne's marriage (1805) with Lady Caroline Ponsonby, the only daughter of the Earl of Bessborough, was a sheer disaster. For twenty years he endured with rare patience and courage the miseries of marriage with a woman of ungovernable temper, who, according to the testimony of a kinsman, was "inordinately vain and excitable to the verge of insanity." Lady Caroline was, for a while, passionately infatuated with Lord Byron, but Melbourne treated her, on the whole, with a consideration, a kindness, even a tenderness, which she little deserved and ill requited. After twenty years of domestic misery the ill-assorted couple separated (1825), and in 1827 Lady Caroline fortunately died.

One thing only Melbourne owed to his marriage: the tantrums of his wife drove him to seek the seclusion of his library, the companionship of his books. He had a seat in the House of Commons, with only four years' interval, from 1806 until his succession to the peerage (1829); he went much into general society, but, until he took office, as Chief Secretary for Ireland under Canning (1827), his main preoccupation was study. He read widely and deeply, especially in classics and theology. "Being a very good Greek scholar," writes Greville, he "has compared the Evidences and all modern Theological works with the writings of the Fathers." According to a noted sceptic of that day, his studies and reflections "led him to a perfect *conviction* of unbelief"; but that statement lacks confirmation.

As his mother's son Melbourne naturally entered the House of Commons as an adherent of the Whig party; but, though his views remained essentially Liberal to the end of his days, he found no difficulty in taking office under Canning, and, what was more remarkable, under the Duke of Wellington. With other Canningites he resigned in 1828, and in the following year, on his father's death, he went to the House of Lords.

On the formation of Lord Grey's "Reform" Government in 1830 Melbourne accepted office as Home Secretary, and an admirable Home Secretary he made. The times were difficult. There was in Ireland (for which the Home Secretary was then responsible) grave disorder, and a good deal of rioting in the southern counties of England. Melbourne displayed a combination of coolness and firmness which rendered the agitators ridiculous and, as far as this country was concerned, dissipated all serious danger. Yet there had been awkward corners to negotiate, notably during the "reform riots" in Bristol and other cities, and

Melbourne's imperturbable temper was a great asset to his colleagues and to the country.

The situation in Ireland was of a much graver character, and it was on the Irish rocks that the Grey Ministry ultimately foundered. For a successor to the Whig veteran King William IV turned to Lord Melbourne, but suggested that he should strengthen a rather weak team by a coalition with Peel and Wellington. Melbourne did not like the idea. Wellington and Peel liked it even less; so the Grey Ministry was patched up under Lord Melbourne as Prime Minister. But after a precarious existence of exactly four months it was suddenly dismissed by the King: "kicked out," as Greville bluntly says, "in the simplest sense of that phrase." Such was, indeed, the prevalent impression at that time, but it is now clear that Melbourne was rather more than a consenting party to his dismissal. One of his biographers goes, indeed, so far as to say that "the King did what his Minister invited him to do." Be that as it may, two things are certain: that the King, mistrustful of the ecclesiastical policy of his Ministers, was anxious to be rid of them; and that the Prime Minister was not sorry to be free of the troubles which he saw ahead of him, particularly in Ireland.

Peel and Wellington came in; but, instead of meeting Parliament, appealed to the new electorate. Peel's famous "Tamworth Manifesto," issued to his constituents in the course of the election, is generally held to have laid the foundations of the "new Conservative" Party. But the new electorate was not yet educated up to the new Conservatism; Peel consequently found himself in a minority in the new House, and, after a few months of office, was beaten on the Irish Tithe question. Melbourne came back into office (1835), but for the next five years Daniel O'Connell was in power.

Some two years after Melbourne's return to office William IV died and Queen Victoria reigned in his stead. At the time of her accession Melbourne was a man of fifty-eight; but it was then that the real work of his life began.

The young Princess, now called to the throne under the style and title of Queen Victoria, was born at Kensington Palace on May 24, 1819. Her father was Edward Augustus, the fourth of the seven sons, the fifth of the thirteen children of George III. Her mother was Victoria Mary Louisa, a daughter of Francis, Duke of Saxe-Coburg-Saalfeld (afterwards Gotha), and widow of Emich Charles, the reigning Prince of Leiningen, who had died in 1814. Princess Charlotte, the eldest grandchild of George III, died in 1817. Of the six younger sons of the old king not one had a legitimate child or even a legal wife. His surviving daughters were either unmarried or childless. The succession to the throne became, therefore, a matter of instant importance, and marriages were arranged, in hot haste, for the Dukes of Clarence, Kent and Cambridge —his three unmarried sons. The marriages all took place in 1818. The Duke of Kent, then in his fifty-second year, had been for years happily though morganatically married, and insisted that his patriotic sacrifice in contracting a legal marriage should be suitably rewarded by Parliament. Though he had been in receipt of £12,000 a year since 1799, his pecuniary position was one of hopeless embarrassment, nor did the additional £6,000 a year, voted to him by Parliament on his legal marriage, suffice to redeem it. Though careless in money matters he was not devoid of proper patriotic pride, and when it was known that the Duchess was with child he insisted on bringing her to England in order that their child should be born on English soil.

The Princess was ushered into the world with the ceremony due to a baby in the direct line of succession. No fewer than five Privy Councillors were summoned to Kensington Palace to attest so important an event, among them the Duke of Sussex, the Duke of Wellington and George Canning. The child was baptized on June 24, 1819, by the names of Alexandrina Victoria, the Czar Alexander being one of her three sponsors.

Of her father the Princess had no recollection; he died less than a week before his own father, George III, in January 1820. The Duke of Kent was a keen soldier—a fact frequently recalled by his daughter—and a kindly man of enlightened views and liberal sympathies. But he died, as he had lived, deeply in debt, and but for the timely generosity of her brother, Prince Leopold of Saxe-Coburg (who, but for the death of his wife, the Princess Charlotte, would have become Prince Consort), the Duchess of Kent and her little daughter would have been in a position of serious embarrassment. Until his acceptance of the Belgian throne (1831) Prince Leopold continued to make his home in England, and devoted himself to the care of his widowed sister and the education of her child. He was rewarded by the warm and constant affection of the Princess, who looked upon him almost as a father. The long series of letters which passed between them proves how well her affection and confidence were justified. In 1827 the Duke of York died without children; George IV died, also childless, in 1830, and on the accession of the Duke of Clarence as William IV the Princess Victoria became heiress-presumptive to the throne. Parliament, thereupon, voted to the Duchess of Kent an extra £10,000 a year, and nothing was neglected to prepare the Princess for the position to which she was now manifestly destined.

Her education was undertaken largely by the Duchess, who was a woman of strong, not to say stern character, and trained her daughter, from the earliest years, in habits of order, punctuality, and obedience. The Duchess was assisted by Fräulein Lehzen, daughter of a Hanoverian pastor, and by the Rev. George Davys, afterwards Bishop of Peterborough. Miss Lehzen, though a stern disciplinarian, won the child's affection, nor did the pupil forget in after years the debt she owed to her preceptress.

Over these years we need not linger; the story has been often told; best of all by the Queen herself, in her *Reminiscences* (written in 1872), and printed by the editors of the Queen's *Letters* (Vol. I) from the original manuscript at Windsor. One or two citations will accordingly suffice.

"I was brought up very simply—never had a room to myself till I was nearly grown up—always slept in my mother's room till I came to the Throne. At Claremont, and in the small houses at the bathing places, I sat and took my lessons in my governess's bedroom. I was not fond of learning as a little child, and baffled every attempt to teach me my letters up to five years old, when I consented to learn them by their being written down before me. I remember going to Carlton House when George IV lived there, as quite a little child, before a dinner the King gave. The Duchess of Cambridge and my two cousins, George and Augusta, were there.

". . . In the year 1826 (I think) George IV asked my mother, my sister, and me down to Windsor for the first time; he had been on bad terms with my poor father when he died, and took hardly any notice of the poor widow and little fatherless girl, who were so poor at the time of his (the Duke of Kent's) death that they could not have travelled back to Kensington Palace had it not been for the kind assistance of my dear uncle, Prince Leopold.

We went to Cumberland Lodge, the King living at the Royal Lodge. . . .

". . . When we arrived at the Royal Lodge the King took me by the hand saying, 'Give me your little paw.' He was large and gouty, but with a wonderful dignity and charm of manner. . . . Then he said he would give me something for me to wear, and that was his picture set in diamonds, which was worn by the Princesses as an Order attached to a blue ribbon on the left shoulder. I was very proud of this. . . .

"Then we went (I think the next day) to Virginia Water, and met the King in his phaeton, in which he was driving the Duchess of Gloucester, and he said, 'Pop her in,' and I was lifted in and placed between him and Aunt Gloucester, who held me round the waist. (Mamma was much frightened.) I remember that I looked with great respect at the scarlet liveries. . . . The King paid great attention to my sister,[1] and some people fancied he might marry her! ! ! She was very lovely then—about eighteen—and had charming manners, about which the King was extremely particular."

This visit to Windsor naturally made a great impression on the child. It was a break in the monotony of a very simple life, and was also the first sign of a reconciliation between the King and the Duchess of Kent. Relations between them, never cordial, had up to this time been strained almost to the breaking-point. The Duchess of Clarence—afterwards Queen Adelaide—treated the Princess and her mother with consistent kindness, but an anxious mother might well think that the less her child saw of the Courts of either of her uncles, the better. But we anticipate. "I also remember," continues the Queen, " going

[1] The Queen's half-sister, the Princess Feodore of Leiningen, afterwards Princess of Hohenlohe.

to see Aunt Augusta at Frogmore, where she lived always in the summer. We lived in a very plain, simple manner: breakfast was at half-past eight; luncheon at half-past one; dinner at seven—to which I came generally when it was no regular large dinner-party—eating my bread and butter out of a small silver basin. Tea was only allowed as a great treat in later years. . . . Up to my fifth year I had been very much indulged by every one, and set pretty well all at defiance. . . . I was naturally very passionate, but always most contrite afterwards. I was taught from the first to beg my maid's pardon for any naughtiness or rudeness towards her; a feeling I have ever retained, and think every one should own their fault in a kind way to any one, be he or she the lowest, if one has been rude to or injured them by word or deed, especially those below you. People will readily forget an insult or an injury when others own their faults, and express sorrow or regret at what they have done."

So the years of childhood passed, and they were hardly ended when in the early hours of June 20, 1837, William IV died at Windsor, and the Princess Victoria was Queen. Only a fortnight earlier had "lessons stopped."

Her uncle Leopold, now King of the Belgians, had given the Princess precise instructions as to the course she was to follow directly King William's death should occur. About that she had, as we shall see, already made up her own mind.

Directly after the old King's death at Windsor, the Archbishop of Canterbury (Dr. Howley), and Lord Conyngham, the Lord Chamberlain, set off post-haste for Kensington. They reached the Palace about five o'clock. Admitted after long delay, they requested an immediate audience. To this request there was some not unnatural demur. But messengers on such a mission were not to be baulked of its fulfilment by ordinary conventionalities. The sequel can be told only in the Queen's own words :—

Tuesday, June 20, 1837.

"I was awoke at six o'clock by mamma, who told me that the Archbishop of Canterbury and Lord Conyngham were here and wished to see me. I got out of bed and went into my sitting-room (only in my dressing-gown), and *alone*, and saw them. Lord Conyngham (the Lord Chamberlain) then acquainted me that my poor uncle the King was no more, and had expired at twelve minutes past two this morning, and consequently that I am Queen. Lord Conyngham knelt down and kissed my hand, at the same time delivering to me the official announcement of the poor King's demise. . . . Since it has pleased Providence to place me in this station, I shall do my utmost to fulfil my duty towards my country. I am very young, and, perhaps, in many, though not in all things, inexperienced, but I am sure that very few have more real goodwill and more real desire to do what is fit and right than I have. . . .

. . . At nine came Lord Melbourne, whom I saw in my room, *and of course quite alone*, as I shall *always* do all my Ministers. He kissed my hand, and I then acquainted him that it had long been my intention to retain him and the rest of the present Ministry at the head of affairs, and that it could not be in better hands than his. He again then kissed my hand. He then read to me the declaration which I was to read to the Council, which he wrote himself, and which is a very fine one. I then talked with him some little time longer, after which he left me. He was in full dress. I like him very much, and feel confidence in him. He is a very straightforward, honest, clever, and good man. . . . At about 11 Lord

Melbourne came again to me, and spoke to me upon various subjects. At about half-past 11 I went downstairs and held a Council in the red saloon.

I went in, of course, quite alone, and remained seated the whole time. My two uncles, the Dukes of Cumberland and Sussex, and Lord Melbourne conducted me. . . . I was not at all nervous, and had the satisfaction of hearing that people were satisfied with what I had done and how I had done it."

Satisfied, indeed, people were, and not a little astonished, as we learn from the account of the scene given by Greville, who was Clerk of the Council from 1821 to 1859, and whose *Journal* is accepted as one of the most valuable, not to add most entertaining, original authorities for this period. Of the Queen's first Council he writes:

"Never was anything like the first impression she produced, or the chorus of praise and admiration which is raised about her manner and behaviour, and certainly not without justice. It was very extraordinary, and something far beyond what was looked for. Her extreme youth and inexperience, and the ignorance of the world concerning her, naturally excited intense curiosity to see how she would act on this trying occasion, and there was a considerable assemblage at the Palace, notwithstanding the short notice which was given. . . . The Lord President informed them of the King's death and suggested that as they were so numerous, that a few of them should repair to the presence of the Queen and inform her of the event. . . . The Queen received them in the adjoining room alone. As soon as they had returned, the proclamation was read and the usual order passed, when the doors were thrown open and the Queen entered accompanied by her two uncles, who advanced to meet her. She bowed to the Lords, took her seat, and then read her speech in a clear, distinct, and audible voice, and without any appearance of fear or embarrassment. She was quite plainly dressed, and in mourning.

After she had read her speech, and taken and signed the oath for the security of the Church of Scotland, the Privy Councillors were sworn, the two Royal Dukes (of Cumberland and Sussex) first, by themselves; and as these two old men, her uncles, knelt before her, swearing allegiance and kissing her hand, I saw her blush up to the eyes, as if she felt the contrast between their civil and their natural relations, and this was the only sign of emotion which she evinced. Her manner to them was very graceful and engaging—she kissed them both, and rose from her chair and moved towards the Duke of Sussex, who was farthest from her and too infirm to reach her. She seemed rather bewildered at the multitude of men who were sworn, and who came one after another to kiss her hand, but she did not speak to anybody, nor did she make the slightest difference in her manner, or show any in her countenance, to any individual of any rank, station, or party. I particularly watched her when Melbourne and the Ministers and the Duke of Wellington and Peel approached her. She went through the whole ceremony—occasionally looking at Melbourne for instructions when she had any doubt what to do, which hardly ever occurred—with perfect calmness and self-possession, but, at the same time, with a graceful modesty and propriety, particularly interesting and ingratiating. When the business was done, she retired as she had entered."

Such was the auspicious opening of the new reign. In the extract from the Queen's *Journal* the italicized words are underlined in the manuscript and are remarkably indicative of the firmness and calm resolution with which this girl of eighteen was facing the task awaiting her. "*Of course quite alone*, as I shall *always* do all my Ministers." Not many hours a Queen, she had already laid down for herself definite rules of conduct and marked out a distinct line of policy. There was to be no interference in matters of State on the part of those nearest and dearest to her —not even of her mother nor of Baroness Lehzen, who remained in her service as private secretary for purely domestic affairs, but was not to touch politics. The limitation was loyally observed by the governess. So a political Private Secretary had to be found.

The office of Private Secretary dates only from 1812, when the Prince Regent raised a constitutional storm by appointing as his Private Secretary a certain Colonel M'Mahon. Purists detected in this new arrangement an insidious attempt to circumvent the constitutional responsibility of the Ministers of the Crown. Was not the Secretary of State the King's Secretary, and was it not his duty in that capacity to wait upon the King? The storm was allayed, but the fact that it arose is significant of the suspicions, not then wholly obliterated, against any semblance of personal monarchy. The matter was evidently one of special importance and delicacy in the case of an inexperienced girl-Queen; much discussion about it took place, but the difficulty was happily solved by the self-sacrifice and devotion of Melbourne, who himself undertook the duties of Private Secretary in addition to those of Prime Minister. This meant that he spent about six hours a day in the company of the Queen, and practically made his home at Windsor and Buckingham Palace. It is difficult to say whether the arrangement gave greater satisfaction to pupil or mentor. One thing is certain, that for the country it was a piece of singular good fortune that in the first years of her reign the Queen should have had at hand an adviser so experienced, so sagacious and personally acceptable, as Lord Melbourne. To the training and guidance of his young sovereign Lord Melbourne practically devoted the remainder of his working days. Nor could any task have been more congenial to himself.

"It was in this new sphere," wrote Sir Henry Bulwer, "for which Providence seemed to have created and educated him, that his various qualities, talents and acquirements were most usefully exercised and most eminently displayed. Had he been merely a dry, matter-of-fact man of business, or a mere man of book-acquired knowledge, he would probably have wearied instead of gaining the attention of his royal scholar; had he been a mere man of pleasure, he might have amused and captivated, but he could not have instructed one on whose knowledge of her duties depended in no small degree the fate of millions; had he been a violent party man, he would have entered upon his task with a warped and partial judgment, with democratical tendencies he would have lowered the just influence of the Monarchy; with monarchical tendencies he might have instilled dangerous doctrines into the mind of the Sovereign. But with a lofty equanimity of judgment, he happily combined great charm of manner, great experience of the world, great knowledge acquired from reading and reflection."

No words could better express Lord Melbourne's unique qualifications for the task so unexpectedly thrust upon him. Nor did the Queen fail to appreciate Melbourne's services to her and the country. On the contrary, her letters and journals are full of references to his sagacity and tact, above all to his fatherly kindness to herself and his tender solicitude for her well-being. Thus within a week of her accession she wrote to King Leopold: "I have seen him (Melbourne) now every day, with the exception of Friday, and the more I see him the more confidence I have in him; he is not only a clever statesman and an honest man, but a good and kind-hearted man. . . . He is of the greatest use to me, both politically and privately."

At the Coronation in Westminster Abbey (June 28, 1838) Melbourne's presence and support were evidently a great comfort to the lonely little lady. In her *Journal* under that date she gives a graphic (if not invariably grammatical) account of that memorable day. Only brief extracts are possible: ". . . the crowds of people exceeded what I have ever seen. . . . Their good-humour and excessive loyalty was beyond everything, and I really cannot say *how* proud I feel to be the Queen of *such* a nation. . . . I reached the Abbey amid deafening cheers at a little after half-past eleven. . . . My excellent Lord Melbourne, who stood very close to me throughout the whole ceremony, was *completely* overcome at this moment [when the Crown was placed on her head and the Peers and Peeresses simultaneously put on their coronets] and very much affected; he gave me *such* a kind and I may say *fatherly* look. . . . When Lord Melbourne's turn to do homage came there was loud cheering. They also cheered Lord Grey and the Duke of Wellington. It's a pretty ceremony. They first of all touch the Crown, and then kiss my hand. When my good Lord Melbourne knelt down and kissed my hand he pressed my hand, and I grasped his with all my heart (*sic*), at which he looked up with his eyes filled with tears, and seemed much touched, as he was, I observed, throughout the whole ceremony."

TOUCHED

It was after six o'clock when the Queen reached the Palace, having left it at ten, "really *not* feeling tired." But Lord Melbourne was, and "took a glass of wine!"

In the evening Lord Melbourne was included in the family dinner-party. He congratulated the Queen "on this most brilliant day, and that all had gone off so well. . . . My kind Lord Melbourne was much affected in speaking of the whole ceremony . . . sitting near me the whole evening. . . . I said to Lord Melbourne when I first sat down that I felt a little tired on my feet. 'You must be very tired,' he said. Spoke of the weight of the Robes, etc., the Coronets; and he turned round to me with the tears in his eyes, and said *so* kindly: 'And you did it beautifully—every part of it, with so much taste; it's a thing that you can't give a person advice upon; it must be left to a person.' To hear this, from this kind impartial friend, gave me a great and real pleasure."

Nevertheless, great as was the Queen's affection for Melbourne and carefully as she attended to his lessons in constitutional procedure, her mentor detected in his pupil the signs of a "peremptory disposition." This was, indeed, strikingly manifested when, in May 1839, Lord Melbourne's Ministry resigned. A Bill for the suspension of the Constitution of Jamaica was, on second reading, carried (May 6) by a majority of only five votes, and the Ministry, beset by difficulties both in Parliament and in Ireland, resigned. The resignation of her first Prime Minister caused, not unnaturally, acute pain to the girl-Queen; nor did she endeavour to conceal it from either the outgoing or the incoming Ministers. To Melbourne she wrote in the midst of the crisis (May 8, 1839) a pathetic little note: "The Queen thinks Lord Melbourne may possibly wish to know how she is this morning; the Queen is somewhat calmer; she was in a wretched state till nine o'clock last night, when she tried to occupy herself and to think less gloomily of this dreadful change . . . but on waking this morning, all—all that had happened in one short eventful day came most forcibly to her mind and brought back her grief. . . ." Melbourne's reply was bracing and eminently sensible: "The situation is very painful, but it is necessary for your Majesty to be prudent and firm. It is of all things necessary not to be suspected of any unfair dealing."

The Queen steeled herself to send for the Duke, who persuaded her to confide the formation of a Ministry to Peel. But both to Peel and to Wellington she ingenuously confessed her confidence in Lord Melbourne, "who had been to her quite a parent." So far so good: but she proceeded (her own account of the interview is written to Lord Melbourne): "The Queen then mentioned her intention to prove her great fairness to her new Government in telling them, that they might know there was no unfair dealing, that I meant to see you often as a friend as I owed so much to you." The confusion of persons is proof of the agitated feelings of the writer. Her first impressions of Peel are confided to Melbourne in the same letter and in not less agitated strain: "The Queen don't like his manner after—Oh! how different, how dreadfully different, to that frank, open, natural and most kind manner of Lord Melbourne. . . . The Queen was very much collected and betrayed no agitation during these two trying audiences. But afterwards again *all* gave way."

For the moment the dreaded separation was averted by the emergence of the famous "Bedchamber Question." Peel insisted, with perfect constitutional propriety, if not too tactfully, that the highest Court officials, female as well as male, must change with the Government. The Queen flatly declined to part with her Whig ladies; Peel stood firm; so Melbourne had to be recalled. The Queen was in high spirits "at having got out of the hands of people who would have sacrificed every personal feeling and instinct of the Queen's to their bad party purposes."

This was manifestly unfair, and sixty years later Queen Victoria confessed to Sir Arthur Bigge (afterwards Lord Stamfordham): "I was very young then, and perhaps I should act differently if it was all to be done again." As a fact, when Peel, two years later, came into power, the Queen, as we shall see, very quickly overcame her dislike to the "cold, odd man," and bestowed upon him her confidence in a degree enjoyed by no other Minister of the reign, except Disraeli.

Peel's stiff attitude on the Bedchamber question was doubtless accentuated by a recent and embarrassing incident. In January 1839, Lady Flora Hastings, lady-in-waiting to the Duchess of Kent, was, owing to her appearance, most improperly suspected by some of the Court ladies of immorality. Both the Queen and the Duchess indignantly repudiated the suggestion; but the matter was referred to Melbourne, who advised that the lady should be examined by Sir James Clark, the royal physician. The examination proved that Lady Flora was suffering from a fatal internal disease from which she died in the ensuing July.

Meanwhile, the matter was taken up by Lady Flora's brother, the Marquis of Hastings, who personally interviewed the Queen, and by his mother, who wrote to Her Majesty passionately demanding the dismissal of Sir James Clark. The scandal was noised abroad; Lady Hastings published in the newspapers her correspondence with the Queen and the Prime Minister: Clark publicly defended his own conduct, and denied the imputations upon him. The public were violently excited; one Tory newspaper went so far as to proclaim Lady Flora to be "the victim of a depraved court"; not a few people were persuaded that the whole incident was the work of the detested "German Camarilla" entrenched in the royal palace. In particular, the shafts of an outraged English aristocracy were levelled at the Baroness Lehzen—probably unjustly. Greville noted (March 2, 1839) that "the Court is plunged in shame and mortification at the exposure . . . while the whole proceeding is looked upon by society at large as to the last degree disgusting and disgraceful." To say as he did (March 25) that "nobody cares for the Queen, her popularity has sunk to zero, and loyalty is a dead letter," was a palpable exaggeration: but that nobody cared for the Government was true.

The Queen might rejoice at her escape from the detested Tories, but despite the recasting of his Cabinet, Melbourne found it increasingly difficult to maintain his parliamentary position. Moreover, the Queen had now less need of him: she had found another confidential adviser. The question of her marriage had naturally engaged attention, and several possible candidates for the position of Queen's Consort had been considered. In October 1839, however, two young cousins of the Queen, Princes Ernest and Albert of Saxe-Coburg, arrived on a visit to Windsor. Their uncle, King Leopold, had long ago decided that his niece should marry Prince Albert. His wish was fulfilled. On October 15, the Queen having herself conceived an overpowering affection for Prince Albert, offered him marriage. "He would never have presumed to take such a liberty as to propose to the Queen of England." So she told the Duchess of Gloucester.[1] The result was satisfactory. "He seems perfection," wrote the Queen to King Leopold, "and I think I have the prospect of very great happiness before me. I *love* him *more* than I can say; and I shall do everything in my power to render the sacrifice he has made (for a *sacrifice* in my opinion it is) as small as I can." She did.

The marriage took place on February 10, 1840. The

[1] *Peel Papers*, II, 414.

Tories had cut down the allowance proposed for the Prince from £50,000 to £30,000 a year, thus deepening the repugnance already felt towards them by the Queen: but Melbourne's tenure was very insecure; nor was he any longer indispensable to the Queen. The Prince Consort soon replaced him as Private Secretary. Moreover, genuine as was the Queen's regard for him, she was quite capable of spirited rebuke when the Prime Minister kept her tardily informed of ministerial changes, or neglected her social commands. Thus, having got him safely back again, she writes (August 26, 1839):

"The Queen . . . thinks it right and of importance that Lord Melbourne should be here at large dinners; the Queen insists upon his coming to dinner to-morrow, and also begs him to do so on Wednesday. . . . The Queen has been a good deal annoyed this evening at Normanby's telling her that John Russell was coming to town next Monday to change with him [as Home Secretary]. Lord Melbourne never told the Queen that this was definitely settled. . . . The Queen has such unlimited confidence in Lord Melbourne that she knows all that he does is right, but she cannot help being a little vexed at not being told things, when she is accustomed to great confidence on Lord Melbourne's part."

Melbourne's tale was, however, nearly told. Not since 1835 had the Whigs been really masters in their own parliamentary house. Six humiliating years of office they had endured, without ever tasting the sweets of power. The position was, indeed, aptly summarized by the Liberal member for Westminster: "The Right Honourable member for Tamworth [Peel] governs England; the honourable and learned member for Dublin [O'Connell] governs Ireland; the Whigs govern nothing but Downing Street." The diagnosis was accurate. In May 1841 the Government was defeated on the Budget. Parliament was dissolved in June, and the country gave the Tories a majority of eighty. The General Election of 1841 was as fatal to the Repealers in Ireland as it was to the Whigs in England. Melbourne resigned, and did his utmost to reconcile the Sovereign to her new Ministers. His success may be counted as his final act of chivalry and service to his Queen and country.

To Peel himself he gave (indirectly through Greville) some kindly and sagacious advice, as to his relations with the Queen: "Don't let him suffer any appointment he is going to make to be talked about, and don't let her hear it through anyone but himself, and whenever he does anything or has anything to propose, let him explain to her clearly his reason. The Queen is not conceited; she is aware there are many things she cannot understand, and she likes to have them explained to her elementarily, not at length and in detail, but shortly and clearly; neither does she like long audiences—I never stayed with her a long time. These things he [Peel] should attend to and they will make things go on more smoothly."

They did. The Queen, as already mentioned, had got a new Private Secretary; she soon gave her full confidence to her new Prime Minister. Of the Prince's "judgment, temper and discretion," Melbourne formed "the highest opinion," and, on relinquishing office, he assured his mistress that he felt "a great consolation and security in the reflection that he left the Queen in a situation in which she had the inestimable advantage of such advice and assistance."

Lord Melbourne continued to lead the Opposition in the House of Lords until, in October 1842, he was prostrated by a stroke of paralysis; but he so far recovered as to be able, during the crisis of 1846, to attend a meeting of Peers at Lansdowne House. To the total repeal of the

Corn Laws Melbourne was opposed, and he considered that their alteration, which he approved, should be done "deliberately and not under excitement." The Whigs were temperamentally averse to excitement and popular agitation, but the counsel was none the less wise. When Peel actually proposed total repeal, Melbourne could not restrain his indignation: "Ma'am, it's a damned dishonest thing," was his famous comment to the Queen. The vigour of his language on that occasion was a reversion to type. Previous to 1837 his conversation had been punctuated with oaths, and it speaks wonders for his self-restraint that after he became the great Queen's Private Secretary, he guarded his own lips as carefully as he informed the mind of his pupil.

A final disappointment awaited him in his premature old-age. When, in 1846, Lord John Russell formed his Ministry, no offer of a place was made to Melbourne. Bitterly chagrined though he was, he generously recognized that Lord John had acted for the best: "You have judged me rightly and kindly in making me no offer." Lord John had judged his old colleague's incapacity for further work only too well. Within two years the end came.

Lord Melbourne's work was done, and well done: he had taught Queen Victoria a lesson which none of her predecessors had learnt so successfully—how (in the classic phrase of Thiers) to reign but not to rule. Yet, though responsibility passed from the Crown to its Ministers, Queen Victoria never became a cypher in the Government of her Empire. "The acts, the wishes, the example of the Sovereign in this country are a real power. An immense reverence and tender affection await upon the person of the one permanent and ever faithful guardian of the fundamental conditions of the Constitution." The words are Mr. Gladstone's; and he wrote of what he knew. Succeeding chapters will demonstrate the accuracy of his analysis.

PLACE of Q

By kind permission of the Proprietors of "Punch"

THE LETTER OF INTRODUCTION

CHAPTER III

SIR ROBERT PEEL—THE NEW CONSERVATISM

Queen Victoria was born and bred a Whig. Her father, the Duke of Kent, passed for an advanced Liberal: he spoke in the House of Lords in favour of Catholic Emancipation; he was interested in the advancement of popular education and in the movement for the abolition of slavery. Though she never knew her father, the Queen was loyal to his memory, and was influenced by his opinions. Moreover, her own mentors, as well as the Prince Consort's, derived their views of the English Constitution from the fashionable text-books of that day—chiefly those of Hallam, whose *Constitutional History* was published in 1827, and Sir James Mackintosh (1765–1832). The first volumes of Macaulay's *History* were not published until 1848, but from 1825 onwards his Essays in the *Edinburgh Review* were doing much to popularize the Whig view of constitutional development in England, and doubtless influenced the Queen and her instructors.

Lord Melbourne's Whiggism was less pronounced than that of the historians, who knew more of books but less of men than he did. He had pre-eminently the "cross-bench mind"; he heartily disliked pedants and mistrusted dogmatists. "I wish," he once said, "I was as cocksure of anything as Tom Macaulay is of everything." Had his wish been gratified, he might have had greater success in party leadership, but he would assuredly have been less qualified to guide the steps of the girl-Queen.

Never did his peculiar abilities show to greater advantage than in the difficult task of smoothing the path for his successor. The "bedchamber dispute" had deepened the Queen's prejudice against the Tories. Their successful opposition to the Prince's allowance still further outraged the Queen's feelings. Melbourne was not, indeed, entirely blameless in that matter. Common prudence should have suggested consultation with the leaders of the Opposition, in order to avoid the possibility of open dispute on a matter so closely affecting the dignity of the throne and the feelings of its occupant.

When, however, it became clear that the days of his ministry were numbered, Melbourne spared no efforts to make things as easy as possible both for the Queen and for Sir Robert. He was, by this time, well aware both of the Queen's obstinacy, and of Peel's "doggedness and pertinacity." But he warned the Queen that she must not take the line she did in 1839, "for that nothing but the forbearance of the Tories had enabled himself and his colleagues to support Her Majesty at that time." On the other hand, he was anxious that Peel should be warned not to be impatient, but to give the Queen time to come round; if the Queen felt he was acting fairly by her, she would, Melbourne was sure, meet him in the same spirit.

The Queen had been inclined to send for the Duke of Wellington, but Melbourne dissuaded her. The event fully justified his advice. Peel proved to be as anxious as the Queen to avoid a repetition of the disagreeable incident of 1839. On the principle he could not yield, but to the Prince's Secretary he declared with obvious sincerity: "I would waive every pretension to office, I declare to God, sooner than that my acceptance of it should be attended with any personal humiliation to the Queen."

There was no humiliation for the Queen; nor any

surrender of principle on Peel's part. From 1841, however, it has been an accepted convention that the "great offices of the Court and situations in the Household held by members of Parliament, should be included in the political arrangements made on a change of administration."[1] As regards the Ladies of the Household, the arrangement is that the Mistress of the Robes changes with the Ministry, but the Ladies-in-waiting are appointed and continue in their appointments without regard to their political connections.

The new Parliament met in August 1841. The Melbourne Ministry was defeated in both Houses on Amendments to the Address, though the Duke of Wellington took the opportunity afforded by the debate to pass a high eulogium on Lord Melbourne's services to the Queen. On August 30 the resignation of the Ministry was formally announced to both Houses.

The Queen at once sent for Peel, who formed an exceptionally strong administration.[2]

The Duke of Wellington (though he wanted the Foreign Office) consented to serve in the Cabinet without portfolio, and to lead the House of Lords. Lyndhurst became for the third time Chancellor; Lord Aberdeen (Foreign), Lord Stanley (Colonies), and Sir James Graham (Home), became Secretaries of State, and Mr. Henry Goulburn Chancellor of the Exchequer. For reasons presently to be disclosed,

[1] Cabinet Minute, May 10, 1839.

[2] Sir R. Peel, b. 1788; ed. Harrow and Christ Church; Tory M.P. for Cashel (1809); Under-Secretary for War and Colonies under Liverpool (1810–12); Chief Secretary for Ireland (1812–18); M.P. for Oxford University (1817); Home Secretary (1822–7); Home Secretary and Leader of H. of C. under Wellington (1828–30); M.P. Westbury (1829), Tamworth (1830–50); P.M. and Ch. of Ex. (1834–5), P.M. (1841–6); d. 1850.

there was more than the usual amount of reconstruction during the five years of Peel's Ministry. Among the younger recruits thus introduced into the Cabinet were two destined to eminence: Mr. Sidney Herbert and Mr. Gladstone. But however able his colleagues, Peel was Prime Minister in more than name. For some years past he had been the foremost figure in the House of Commons: as a debater, second only to Stanley, "the Rupert of debate"; as an administrator, without a rival. In the Cabinet his supremacy was unquestioned, and he exercised over every department a personal supervision such as no Prime Minister has exercised before or since. Sir James Graham was his chief lieutenant, but no one more clearly recognized Peel's unique position: "We never had a Minister who was so truly a First Minister as he is. He makes himself felt in every department, and is really cognizant of the affairs of each." Thus wrote Graham. "You have been Prime Minister," wrote Gladstone to Peel in 1846, "in a sense in which no other man has been since Mr. Pitt's time." Lord Rosebery goes further. Peel, he said, was "the model of all Prime Ministers. It is more than doubtful, indeed, if it be possible in this generation, when the burdens of Empire and Office have so incalculably grown, for any Prime Minister to discharge the duties of his high post with the same thoroughness or in the same spirit as Peel. . . . Peel kept a strict supervision over every department: he seems to have been master of the business of each and all of them . . . it is probable that no other Prime Minister ever fulfilled so completely and thoroughly the functions of his office, parliamentary, administrative, and general, as Sir Robert Peel." But Peel himself was evidently conscious that his own conception of his office was becoming impossible of realization, except by sending all Prime Ministers to the House of Lords—

a solution to which he personally refused to assent. "I defy the Minister of this country," he wrote in August 1845, "to perform properly the duties of his office . . . to keep up the constant communication with the Queen, *and the Prince* [the italics are Peel's] . . . and also sit in the House of Commons eight hours a day for 118 days." The duty of correspondence with the Sovereign is naturally a heavy one. Lord Salisbury once answered a sympathetic inquiry as to how he bore the burden of his two offices with some petulance: "I could do very well with two departments; in fact, I have four—the Prime Ministership, the Foreign Office, the Queen, and Randolph Churchill —and the burden of them increases in that order." No one, as will be seen, had a higher appreciation of the Queen's devotion to duty than Lord Salisbury; but there were moments when he was impatient of the strain his office imposed on him. Peel's italics show that, in his case, the strain was increased by the necessity of explaining things twice. But, nevertheless, he and the Prince were quickly drawn to each other, and excellent relations between them were established and maintained.

Supreme in the House of Commons, master of his Cabinet, Peel had also by 1841 established a strong position in the country. He was associated by birth with that commercial aristocracy which, later on, was to produce other Prime Ministers in the persons of Gladstone, Campbell-Bannerman and Mr. Baldwin. Educated like the last at Harrow, and like the first at Christ Church, he was the first representative of the new ruling class to become Prime Minister.

Another distinction belongs to Peel. Toryism, as he perceived, could not survive the Reform Act of 1832; accordingly he at once set about the task of reconstructing his party. His address to the electors of Tamworth in 1835 laid the foundations of the new Conservatism. The "Tamworth Manifesto" must then be regarded as an historic document.[1] Peel claimed, and justly, that his own record proved that he had never been the "defender of abuses or the enemy of judicious reforms." He definitely accepted the Reform Bill "as a final and irrevocable settlement of a great constitutional question." Nor was he opposed to the spirit of the Act if properly understood and wisely interpreted. But these conditions were essential. "If by adopting the spirit of the Reform Bill it be meant that we are to live in a perpetual vortex of agitation; that public men can only support themselves in public estimation by adopting every popular impression of the day, by promising the instant redress of anything that anybody may call an abuse . . . I will not undertake to adopt it. But if the spirit of the Reform Bill implies merely a careful review of institutions civil and ecclesiastical, undertaken in a friendly temper, combining with the firm maintenance of established rights the correction of proved abuses and the redress of real grievances, in that case I can for myself and my colleagues undertake to act in such a spirit and with such intentions."

The education of the constituencies in the principles of the new Conservatism was, naturally, a work of time. The General Election of 1835 raised the number of Peel's followers from 150 to 270, of whom 230 were Conservatives and 40 were "moderate Whigs." Not until 1841 did the Conservatives find themselves in a clear majority. It then numbered over 80. Peel's parliamentary position was thus assured, but the "cold, shy man" had still to establish himself in the favour of the Court. He succeeded in doing so much more quickly than might have been anticipated. The Queen was deeply

[1] Text in full in *Sir R. Peel's Memoirs*, II, 58 f.

distressed at parting with Lord Melbourne, but was comforted by the latter's tactful reminder that she now had the "inestimable advantage" of a "confidential counsellor constantly at her side," and that he had formed "the highest opinion" of the Prince's "judgment, temper and discretion."

That discretion was evidently lacking when the Prince urged Lord Melbourne to maintain his correspondence with the Queen despite the change of Ministry. Melbourne unwisely acceded to the request, to the increasing alarm and indignation of Baron Stockmar.

Stockmar, a native of Coburg, had originally been brought to England in 1816 as his medical attendant by Prince Leopold. He was a man of high character and great intelligence. Even Palmerston, who disliked his German priggishness, admitted that he was the most disinterested man he ever met. A diligent student of the English Constitution, he was selected by King Leopold as the person best qualified to instruct the Princess Victoria in that recondite subject, and he remained a member of her household, though in an unofficial capacity, throughout the years 1837–8. In 1839 King Leopold sent him with the young Prince Albert on a tour to Italy. Stockmar was entrusted with a twofold duty: to keep the mind and heart of Prince Albert constant to his cousin in England, and to instruct him in the history and conventions of the English Constitution. Both duties having been successfully discharged, Stockmar resumed his residence at the English Court, and after the Queen's marriage continued as the highly trusted but unofficial adviser of both the Queen and the Prince Consort. In 1857 he retired to Coburg, where he died in 1863.

After the accession of Peel to office, Stockmar took Melbourne to task for continuing (albeit at her urgent request) his correspondence and intercourse with the Queen. The point thus raised was, and is, one of extreme delicacy. Is the Sovereign entitled to seek the advice of persons other than Ministers? The point was again raised, as we shall see, in January 1886, when the Queen pressed Mr. (afterwards Viscount) Goschen to go to Osborne for a personal consultation. He begged to be excused on the ground that his visit would "expose the action of your Majesty to much misconstruction and misrepresentation." The Queen demurred to his objections and quoted against him the precedent (among others) of 1851 where, during the ministerial crisis that ensued on the defeat of Lord John Russell, she consulted the Duke of Wellington. Mr. Goschen, though maintaining his previous attitude, was fain to admit that "your Majesty is constitutionally entitled to consult anyone on an occasion such as this in whom your Majesty places confidence." "Anyone" puts it too broadly. Sir William Anson seems to limit the right of consultation to peers. The Sovereign, he says, "has a right to demand, and any peer . . . has a right to offer counsel on matters which are of importance to the public welfare." Mr. Gladstone, commenting at a much later date (1876) upon the attacks made upon the Prince Consort on the eve of the Crimean War, wrote: "It was a matter of course that the Queen's husband should be more or less her political adviser. It would have been nothing less than a violence done to nature if, with his great powers and congenial will, any limits had been placed upon the relations of confidence between the two, with respect to any public affairs whatever. . . . We must go further. It does not seem easy to limit the Sovereign's right of taking friendly counsel, by any absolute rule, to the case of a husband. If it is the Queen's duty to form a judgment upon important proposals submitted to her by her Ministers, she has an indisputable right to the use of all instruments which will enable her to discharge that duty with effect; subject always, and subject only, to the one vital condition that they do not disturb the relation, on which the whole machinery of the Constitution hinges, between those Ministers and the Crown. *She cannot, therefore, as a rule, legitimately consult in private on political matters with the party in opposition to the Government of the day.*" [1]

The words italicized seem to justify Stockmar's contention. His memorandum [2] is in form intolerably priggish and pedantic; his fears were probably exaggerated; the letters now published show that Melbourne acted throughout "with scrupulous honour and delicacy, and tried to augment, rather than undermine, Peel's growing influence with the Queen and Prince." Nevertheless, by his courageous remonstrance Stockmar rendered a real service to Peel, and still more to the Sovereign. He insisted that this continued intercourse between the Court and the late Minister was "an essential injustice" to Peel, that it could not continue without exposing the Queen to misrepresentation, and without "creating mighty embarrassments in the finer and regular working of a constitutional machine." He put the case to Melbourne in the bluntest way: "Would you have it said," he wrote, "that Sir Robert Peel failed in his trial merely because the Queen alone was not fair to him, and that principally *you* had aided her in the game of dishonesty?"

As a fact there was no question of dishonesty on the Queen's part, nor of "failure" on Peel's. The Queen very quickly overcame her initial dislike and bestowed upon the new Minister her fullest confidence. Peel was, indeed, confronted by immense difficulties; but they arose from the

[1] *Gleanings*, I, 73. [2] *Q.V.L.*, I, 425 f.

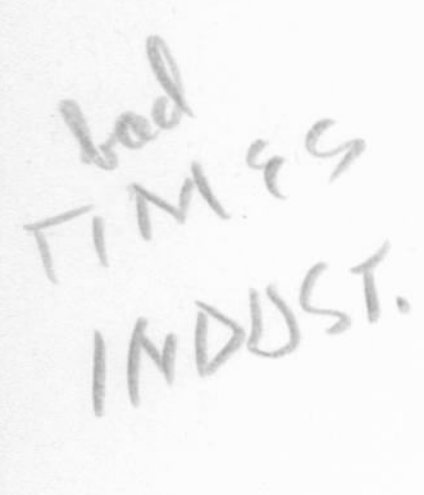

serious condition of the country, not from the attitude of the Court.

The winter of 1841–2 was, in an industrial sense, one of the worst through which this country ever passed. Prices were high; wages were low; factories were closed; iron foundries shut down; from all parts of the country came the same tale of unemployment, distress and actual starvation. Writing under the date November 2, 1842, Greville says:

"Lord Wharncliffe and Kay Shuttleworth, who are both come from the north, have given me an account of the state of the country and of the people which is perfectly appalling. There is an immense and continually increasing population, deep distress and privation, no adequate demand for labour, no demand for anything, no confidence, but a universal alarm, disquietude, and discontent. Nobody can sell anything. Somebody said, speaking of some part of Yorkshire, 'This is certainly the happiest country in the world, *for nobody wants anything.*' Kay says that nobody can conceive the state of demoralization of the people . . . certainly I have never seen, in the course of my life, so serious a state of things as that which now stares us in the face. . . . One remarkable feature in the present condition of affairs is that nobody can account for it."

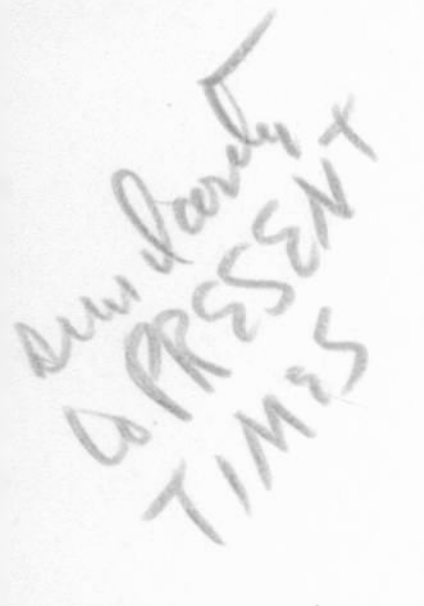

That was not the only feature in which the crisis of 1841 resembled that of our own time (1930–3).

To the free-trade doctrines proclaimed by Cobden and Bright, Peel was himself gradually converted. It was his main political achievement to give them legislative effect.

Between 1841 and 1846 Peel carried through a fiscal revolution which determined for all time to come the fate of his country. Down to the 'forties there had been maintained, despite the industrial changes of the previous half-century, a reasonable balance between agriculture and industry, between the countryside and the towns. British farmers could still feed—at a price—the workers in the new towns, in mines, and factories. Thenceforward, statesmen of all parties devoted their attention to the towns, to the promotion of industry, shipping, and international trade. Population increased with tremendous rapidity, and was more and more concentrated in the towns; the villages dwindled; agriculture, once the main source of our wealth, was suffered to become the Cinderella among the occupations of our people. Lancashire, the West Riding, and the Lowlands of Scotland were quickly covered with a network of manufacturing towns. The North-eastern Counties, the Midlands, and South Wales were converted into vast coalfields. To attribute all this development to the policy of Peel would be an exaggeration; yet his Ministry marked the decisive turning-point.

When Peel took office the country was sore stricken. He diagnosed the disease as economic, and believed that only by the application of economic remedies could the symptoms be alleviated.

Between 1841 and 1846 he applied them. "We must make this country," he said, "a *cheap* country for living." He went far to make it so. By a series of masterly Budgets he restored order to the finances; on one commodity after another he reduced the customs' duty, on some 500 articles he abolished it altogether. But so skilful was his handling of the problem, so great the impulse to trade, that the revenue suffered little. Duties were reduced or remitted to the amount of £6,000,000, yet the yield in 1847 was only £1,200,000 below the yield of 1841. To meet the deficiency, and provide a surplus, an income tax of 7*d.* in the £ was imposed for three years, and at the end of three years was renewed; the interest on £250,000,000 of the

Consolidated Debt was reduced immediately from 3½ per cent. to 3¼, and ultimately to 3. The Bank Charter Act of 1844 made London the financial capital of the world, and gave to English currency and credit a stability which was never really impaired until 1931.

The climax was reached in 1846. In 1845 a double calamity had fallen on the land: the wheat crop failed in England; the potato crop failed in Ireland. The teeming population of Ireland, then over 8,000,000, was threatened with starvation; the English artisans were in hardly less serious plight. In 1842 Peel had carried a sliding scale for the corn duties. By December 1845 he was convinced that the Corn Laws must be abolished altogether. He was also convinced that if once the ports were opened to foreign food, they would never again be closed.

But was Peel, the leader of the Conservative Party, the trusted spokesman of the "Gentlemen of England," the man to carry through so momentous a revolution? As to the necessity for repeal, total and immediate, he had no longer any doubt, and had decided, when the existing Parliament had run its course, to appeal to the country, free of all party ties and obligations, as a Free Trader. But as the summer of 1845 wore on he began to watch the barometer with ever-deepening anxiety. "The rain it raineth every day." At the end of September alarming reports began to come in from Ireland. Anxious deliberations in the Cabinet ensued. Peel confessed to his colleagues his change of opinion on the Corn Laws, but he held that the enactment of Free Trade should be left to others. But to whom? Only the Cobdenites had declared categorically in favour of it.

On November 27, however, a bombshell exploded. *The Times* published a letter written from Edinburgh by Lord John Russell declaring for total repeal. On December 5

Greville found "political affairs in a state of the greatest interest and excitement." *The Times* had, on the previous day, published the news that the Cabinet had agreed on the total repeal of the Corn Laws. They had; but with dissentients, and on December 5 Peel wrote to the Queen "with a heart full of gratitude and devotion to Her Majesty," but intimating that "in the present state of affairs" he could render more service to her and to the country "in a private than in a public station." His resignation was reluctantly accepted, and the Queen sent for Lord John Russell, who asked for time to consult his colleagues. They proved to be as much divided on the question as was the outgoing Cabinet. Peel chivalrously undertook to support Lord John, but the latter, after a week of hectic negotiations, reported to the Queen his failure to form a Government. In Disraeli's caustic phrase, he "handed back with courtesy the poisoned chalice to Sir Robert."

When Peel arrived at Windsor to take leave, the Queen at once said: "So far from taking leave of you, Sir Robert, I must require you to withdraw your resignation and remain in my service." Peel (according to Prince Albert) was "much affected" and without hesitation promised "to stand by the Queen" and confront the House of Commons if necessary without a single colleague. "I want," he said, "no consultation, no time for reflection. I will be your Minister, happen what may. I will do without a colleague rather than leave you in this extremity." Three days later the Queen wrote to King Leopold: "I have little to add . . . except my extreme admiration of our worthy Peel, who shows himself a man of unbounded *loyalty, courage,* patriotism and *high-mindedness,* and his conduct towards me has been *chivalrous* almost, I might say. I never have seen him so excited or so determined, and *such* a good cause must succeed. We have indeed had an escape. . . ."

All Peel's colleagues stood by him except Lord Stanley, who was succeeded at the Colonial Office by Mr. Gladstone, an arrangement which Peel presciently regarded as "of great importance."

On January 22, 1846, the Queen opened Parliament in person. Peel explained his position in one of the greatest speeches of his life. The Queen's congratulations were profuse. "The Queen," she wrote on January 23, "must congratulate Sir Robert Peel on his beautiful and indeed *unanswerable* speech of last night, which we have been reading with the greatest attention." How fully she realized the sacrifice which Peel was making is clear from a letter (March 3) to King Leopold: "Peel has a very anxious and a very peculiar position, and it is the force of circumstances, and the great energy he *alone possesses*, which will carry him through the session. He certainly acts a most disinterested part, for did he not feel (*as every one* who is fully acquainted with the *real state* of the country must feel) that the line he pursues is the *only right* and sound one for the welfare of this country, he never would have exposed himself to all the annoyance and pain of being attacked by his friends."

Peel's most bitter opponent could hardly be described as a " friend." Disraeli had regarded it as an "intolerable humiliation," not to have been included in Peel's Ministry in 1841, and both he and his wife had written to Peel to say so. Peel's reply was a model of delicacy and courtesy; but Disraeli could not forgive Peel, still less his own undignified indiscretion. The moment for long-meditated revenge had now come.

The episode is described by Disraeli himself in his *Life of Lord George Bentinck* (Chap. III). "The House," he writes, "was on the tenters for the promised detail of the circumstances which had led to the resignation of the Government; they wanted the personal matters . . . Instead of that the bewildered House was listening once more to lucid narratives of the price of flax and wool . . . some dissertation on domestic lard . . . and the importation of foreign cattle. It was, after all, a 'fat cattle' debate again!" Peel was followed by Lord John with the authentic statement of Whig disasters. Then "it seemed that the curtain was about to fall" when "a member who, though on the Tory benches, had been for two sessions in opposition to the Ministry, ventured to rise and attack the Minister. . . . But it was the long-constrained passion of the House that now found a vent far more than the sallies of the speaker that changed the frigid silence of this senate into excitement and tumult."

No wonder there was excitement. In "an hour of gibes and bitterness" Disraeli denounced Peel's speech as a "glorious example of egoistical rhetoric," and his policy as a gross betrayal of the principles which had put him in power and the party which kept him there. The speech, one of Disraeli's most brilliant efforts, must be read in full to be appreciated.[1] It marked the genesis of the new Protectionist Party. But the address was carried without a dissentient.

Five days later Peel unfolded his plan: cheap raw materials for the manufacturer, but no protection against fair foreign competition; cheaper seed for the farmer, but no protection against foreign meat or corn; for all, cheaper living. The Corn Laws were not to be abrogated immediately or totally; the duty was to be reduced to 1*s.* after February 1, 1849; but in the meantime it was to be 10*s.* when the price averaged less than 48*s.* a quarter, diminishing to 4*s.* when it was 53*s.* or over.

[1] E.g. in Kebbel's edition of *Beaconsfield's Speeches*, Vol. I, pp. 98–110.

The Protectionists, led with consummate skill and adroitness by Lord George Bentinck and Disraeli, made a great fight, but Peel carried his Corn Bill through the House of Commons with comparative ease; the Duke of Wellington steered it through the more stormy waters in the Lords, and before the end of June it had become law. The battle was won; but in the moment of victory the general fell.

Throughout the whole crisis the Queen gave her Minister loyal support and constant encouragement. On the merits of the question she had formed a decided opinion, and was at no pains to conceal it. But Peel's enemies were alert to trip him up at the first opportunity. It soon came. On June 25 the Corn Bill was read a third time in the Lords; on the same night the Ministry were defeated in the Commons, on their *Life Preservation Bill* for Ireland, by a majority of 73. The Protectionists could not defeat, nor even materially retard the Corn Bill, but they could take a melodramatic revenge upon its author. Not for the first time, as they maintained, had Peel fouled his own nest, betrayed his principles, and fooled his followers. The majority which defeated him was a composite one: Tories and Whigs, Protectionists and Free Traders, Radicals and Repealers. The alliance was as short-lived as it was infamous: but it sufficed; and to the arch-intriguer the revenge it brought was infinitely sweet. He has himself described the scene on the night of the fatal Division: "Peel sat, lonely and grim, on the Treasury Bench, as the Protectionists passed in defile before the Minister into the hostile lobby. It was impossible that he could have marked them without emotion: the flower of that great party which had been so proud to follow one who was so proud to lead them. . . . They trooped on . . . Sir Robert looked very grave. . . . He began to comprehend his position, and that the Emperor was without an army."

Three days later Peel tendered his resignation to the Queen, and on June 29 announced it to the House in a speech described by Bishop Wilberforce (who heard it) as "very fine; very effective; really almost solemn."

Greville, on the contrary, while admitting that Peel's conduct was admirable, says the speech was "very generally condemned. Almost every part of it offended somebody; but his unnecessary panegyric of Cobden, his allusion to the selfish monopolists, and his claptrap about cheap bread in the peroration exasperated to the last degree his former friends and adherents, were unpalatable to those he has kept, were condemned by all parties indiscriminately, and above all deeply offended the Duke of Wellington."

Anyway, Peel's ministerial career was at an end. But until his life was abruptly terminated by an accident in 1850, he remained, though out of office, undeniably in power. Without his steady support, his successors could never have survived the cross-currents and fierce storms, through which they had to steer their course in Parliament.

From the throne to the cottage Peel's premature death was universally mourned: but of the many noble tributes paid to his memory, perhaps the most felicitous was that of his disciple, Mr. Gladstone, who appropriately quoted Scott's superb lines on Pitt:

> Now is the stately column broke,
> The beacon light is quenched in smoke,
> The trumpet's silver sound is still,
> The warder silent on the hill.
> Hadst thou but lived, tho' stripped of power,
> A watchman on the lonely tower,
> Thy thrilling trump had roused the land
> When fraud and danger were at hand;
> By thee as by the beacon's light,
> Our pilots had kept course aright . . .

The critical judgments passed on Peel's political career are on the whole less divergent than in the case of most politicians. His private life was without reproach, his character of the highest. "I never knew a man in whose truth and justice I had a more lively confidence." Such a tribute from the Duke of Wellington, his closest political associate, must be accepted as conclusive. Disraeli, his most virulent opponent, described him as "the greatest member of Parliament that ever lived . . . a transcendant administrator of public business, and a matchless master of debate. . . . He played upon the House of Commons as upon an old fiddle." Yet Disraeli definitely denied to Peel the gift of originality: "For between forty and fifty years, from the days of Mr. Horner to those of Cobden, he had traded on the ideas and intelligence of others." His life had been "one great appropriation clause," no statesman had "committed petty larceny on so great a scale." This was, of course, the language of debate, exaggerated and unfair; but even in the comparative calm of literary composition Disraeli denied to his great rival the gifts of prescience and originality. He had a "dangerous sympathy with the creations of others"; he lacked the "gift of true leadership"; he was " really deficient in self-confidence"; he was " a bad judge of character and had little knowledge of men." Disraeli was evidently captious and biassed. But even Bagehot, who was neither, makes the same point more delicately when he says that "he was prone to receive the daily deposits of insensibly changing opinion."

Does this constitute condemnation? Is it not rather high testimony to the statesmanship demanded by the peculiar conditions of Parliamentary Democracy? Representative Government calls for a diversity of gifts. Cobden and Bright could arouse popular enthusiasm, but neither could have carried the repeal of the Corn Laws. O'Connell was the most effective mob orator ever returned to St. Stephen's, but he would never have persuaded Parliament to concede Catholic Emancipation. An O'Connell and a Cobden can sow the seed; the Grahams and the Goulburns can water; but to garner the parliamentary harvest calls for the strong will and the clear brain of a Peel.

CHAPTER IV

LORD JOHN RUSSELL—WHIGGISM *IN EXCELSIS*

NEVER in the annals of Parliament has there been a Coalition more incongruous than that which on June 25, 1846, overthrew the Ministry of Sir Robert Peel. Cheek by jowl in the division lobby were Lord George Bentinck and John Bright, Cobden and two Cavendishes, Disraeli and Daniel O'Connell, Lord John Russell and Lord Granby, the scions of many a noble family, Berkeleys, Beresfords, Howards, Manners, and Stanleys, with the Irish rabble that followed O'Connell and the younger Grattan.

But no one could have felt so uncomfortable in that company as the author of the *Edinburgh Letter*, the man who, during the crisis of 1845, had been treated by Peel with peculiar consideration, who was at one with him on the principle of Free Trade, and was now, as the result of a fortuitous and temporary alliance, called upon to succeed him.

From Peel, the Queen and Prince Albert parted with profound regret; nor were they without misgivings as to the competence of his successor to control a difficult situation. Lord John Russell's diminutive stature gave an irresistible chance to the cartoonist, and Mr. *Punch*, as usual, epitomized public opinion in a sentence. The Queen and Prince are interviewing the new "buttons," and the Queen frankly says to him: "I'm afraid you're not strong enough for the place, John." The sequel justified her prescience.

By kind permission of the Proprietors of "Punch"

"I'm afraid you're not strong enough for the place, John."

Lord John Russell belonged by birth to one of the great "revolution families"—a family which from Tudor days had given regular service to the State. Writing in 1841, Lord John claimed that "in all times of popular movement the Russells have been on the 'forward' side." He himself conformed to type; but in one respect he was unique not only among the Russells, but among all the statesmen of the century. In length of political service none could rival him. Born in the year [1] when revolutionary France declared war on Europe (1792), he died in the year when Lord Beaconsfield brought back "peace with honour" from Berlin (1878). He was a member of the Legislature for sixty-five years. Elected to the House of Commons two years before the battle of Waterloo, he had become the recognized spokesman of the "Reform" party before George III died. Admitted to the Cabinet in the second year of William IV, he became leader of the House of Commons two years before the accession of Queen Victoria. He held high office for more than twenty years and was twice Prime Minister.

He formed his first Ministry in 1846. Except the Lord Chancellor (Lord Cottenham) and Macaulay, who was for a few months Paymaster of the Forces, all the members of Russell's Cabinet held office by the Divine right of Whiggism. Eight of the fifteen were hereditary peers, and all the rest, with the exceptions named, were closely

[1] Russell, Lord John, first Earl Russell, b. 1792; ed. Westminster and Edinburgh University; M.P. Tavistock (1813–20); for Huntingdon (1820–6); for Bandon (1826–30); Tavistock (1830–5); Paymaster-General (1831); M.P. Stroud (1835–47); Home Secretary and Leader of H. of C. (1835); Secretary for War and Colonies (1839); M.P. City of London (1847–61); P.M. (1846–52); Foreign Secretary (1852–3); in Cabinet without office (1853–4); President of Council (1854–5); Secretary for Colonies (Feb.–July 1855); Foreign Secretary (1859–66); Earl Russell (1861); P.M. (1865–66); d. 1878.

connected with the Peerage. The Ministry was deficient neither in ability nor experience, but until the summer of 1847, Lord John was in a minority, nor did the General Election of that year give him an absolute majority; the Whigs numbering only 325, the Protectionists 225, and the Conservative Free Traders or "Peelites" 105. Only with the support of the "Peelites," therefore, could Russell retain office. As a fact, he retained it for five more years.

In his financial policy Russell adhered steadfastly to the principles of Peel, but the abolition of the preference on Colonial sugar (1846), though it benefited both the revenue and the consumer, was bitterly resented by the Protectionists. Much more serious, however, was the financial panic which in 1847 ensued on the wild speculation in railway shares. No fewer than 220 great houses failed; consols fell from 95 to 78; the discount rate rose nominally to 8 per cent., and even at that rate money was almost unobtainable. But on October 25 the Government authorized the Bank to infringe its charter of 1844, and issue notes beyond the limits of the gold reserve. The permission itself sufficed. Confidence was restored; the panic subsided. It was, however, on the States of continental Europe that attention was at this moment concentrated. With the turn of the year 1847–8 the flood-gates of revolution were opened.

But it was Ireland that provided the main source of anxiety. Famine and crime stalked hand in hand through the country. The peasants had to be at once succoured and coerced. Peel had been turned out—nominally, at any rate—on his Coercion Bill, but the new Government found the ordinary laws quite inadequate for the repression of crime, and the maintenance of order. Their first business was, however, to save the great mass of the Irish people from starvation. In the summer of 1847 over 3,000,000 people had to be supported by the Government; but by the autumn the worst was over: vast quantities of seed were distributed to the peasants; land acquired by the Government was resold or let on easy terms; expert fish-curers were brought over from Scotland to instruct the Irish fishermen, and after the winter of 1847–8 the menace of famine was dissipated. Meanwhile, about 1,000,000 people had perished, and between 1846 and 1851, 1,000,000 more left the shores of old Ireland to found a new Ireland on the other side of the Atlantic. By 1851 the population, which in 1841 stood at 8,175,124, had diminished to 6,552,385. Russell encouraged emigration, but did not rely solely on that expedient for a solution of the Irish problem. He set up an Encumbered Estates Court to facilitate the transference of land from the ruined landlords to new proprietors. Over 7,000 people acquired in this way a stake in the country; but the new men proved much harder landlords than the old. A new Poor Law was enacted in 1847, and in the same year Peel helped the Government to pass a Coercion Act far more stringent than the one on which he had been defeated. Yet despite the Act, Ireland, under the stimulus of the continental revolutions, broke out into armed insurrection (1848) under the leadership of Smith O'Brien, an Irishman of gentle birth and English breeding. With O'Brien were associated Thomas Francis Meagher, a brilliant young lawyer, who in 1847 had with Gavan Duffy founded the Irish Confederation, and John Mitchel, an Irish journalist. The insurrection fizzled out, and none of the leaders suffered anything worse than transportation—the prelude in two cases to useful and honourable careers in Australia.

So rapid was the improvement in the state of Ireland after the '48, that in August 1849 the Queen, accompanied by the Prince Consort and their elder children, paid her first visit to that part of her dominions. She arrived at the Cove of Cork (renamed Queenstown in honour of the visit), and after visiting Cork proceeded by sea to Dublin and Belfast. The Queen insisted that in view of the "general distress unfortunately still prevalent in Ireland" there should be no such "ill-timed expenditure" as a State visit would involve, but she was delighted with the enthusiasm everywhere displayed. Equally delighted was the Lord-Lieutenant (Clarendon), who wrote to Sir George Grey (Home Secretary): "The Queen's presence . . . has united all classes and parties in a manner incredible to those who know the distance at which they have hitherto been kept asunder. . . . In short, the people are not only enchanted with the Queen and the gracious kindness of her manner and the confidence she has shown in them, but they are pleased with themselves for their own good feelings and behaviour, which they consider have removed the barrier that hitherto existed between the Sovereign and themselves, and that they now occupy a higher place in the eyes of the world."

Once more the "talisman of the royal presence" had been tried in Ireland; and, as usual, not in vain. The greater the pity that the Queen tried it again so seldom. True it is, as Goldwin Smith has said, that while "the Teuton loves laws and parliaments, the Celt loves a King." In the absence of his lawful King he "will crown apes." So Henry VII observed à propos of Lambert Simnel, then a scullion in the royal kitchen, to his guest the Earl of Kildare. The observation intended to be derisive was profoundly true.

Not only in Ireland were the repercussions of the continental revolutions felt. The year 1848 witnessed also the final ebullition of the Chartist movement. Early in the year there had been riots in Glasgow, which, though serious, were without much difficulty suppressed. Feargus O'Connor, whose paper the *Northern Star* was the official organ of Chartism, convened a great meeting to be held on Kennington Common on April 10. Thence a procession carrying a monster petition in favour of the People's Charter was to march to the House of Commons. In view of what was happening in Paris, in Vienna, in Prague, in Milan, Venice and Rome—to mention only a few of the centres of disturbance—there was considerable alarm in London. The procession was prohibited; the Duke of Wellington, placed in command of the metropolis, was prepared for any emergency; a large body of special constables—among whom was Prince Louis Napoleon—was enrolled; but the whole movement ignominiously collapsed; the procession was abandoned; the monster petition reached Palace Yard in a cab; Chartism was laughed out of Court. Yet within two generations all the six "points" of the Charter were, with a single insignificant exception, conceded by the Legislature. Chartism was extinguished; the Charter is the law of the land. That, however, is not the whole story. The real driving force behind the Chartist movement, as behind the February Revolution in France, was less political than economic. But Peel had drawn the fangs of economic discontent. Fiscal reform was making England a cheap country for the wage-earner.

Moreover, in 1847, Lord Ashley (afterwards the Earl of Shaftesbury) and Mr. Fielden, a Lancashire cotton-spinner, carried a Bill for limiting to ten hours the labour of women and children in textile factories. In some quarters the Bill was represented as "the revenge of the landlords upon the manufacturers for reform and free trade"; in others, as "a victory of the people of England over official England." In both statements there was an element of truth; but neither contained the whole truth. The consistent advocates of *laissez-faire* were necessarily opposed to State interference with industry; philanthropists cordially welcomed it; it accorded in principle with the philosophy of Protection.

Worsted in their fight against the Factory Act, the disciples of the Manchester School welcomed the final repeal of the Navigation Laws in 1849, and the Australian Act (1850) which conferred upon the colonies in Australia and New Zealand power to settle their own form of Government. As a result these colonies followed the example of Canada and adopted the principle of "responsible" Government.

The colonial policy of the Manchester School will demand attention later on. For the present it must suffice to note that it was in complete harmony with the *laissez-faire* doctrine which dictated the repeal of Corn Laws and Navigation Laws, which deprived colonial sugar of preference, and opposed factory legislation. Why confine the ideas of brotherhood to British brethren? Why favour our own kith and kin beyond the seas, or protect our agriculturists and industrialists at home? Was there not an identity of economic interests between the peoples of all countries? Throw down the barriers which impeded trade between nation and nation, and the world would enjoy the blessings of perpetual peace.

The apostles of the Manchester School were, in fine, international idealists, and of their principles the great Exhibition of 1851 was the material apotheosis. The idea of the Exhibition was Prince Albert's, and he it was who, in face of prolonged and sometimes bitter opposition, personally superintended the preliminary arrangements upon which success depended.

England was to give a noble example to the world. A banquet at the Mansion House (March 21, 1850) gave the Prince the opportunity of unfolding his scheme to a company which included the leading statesmen of the day, the

Foreign ambassadors, and the chief magistrates of more than two hundred provincial towns. The opportunity was, by general consent, brilliantly redeemed. The Prince made the speech of his life. The Exhibition was to "give a true test and living picture of the point of development at which world-civilization had arrived, and to demonstrate that the blessings bountifully bestowed upon mankind by the Creator could be realized only in proportion to the help which we are prepared to render each other; only by peace, love and ready assistance, not only between individuals but between the nations of the earth."

A "crystal palace" designed by Sir Joseph Paxton was erected to house the exhibits in Hyde Park; and on May 1, 1851, with splendid ceremonial, and amid scenes of tumultuous enthusiasm, the Queen, accompanied by her husband and children, opened the Exhibition. With pardonable exaggeration she described the event to King Leopold as "the greatest day in our history, the most *beautiful* and *imposing* and *touching* spectacle ever seen, and the triumph of my beloved Albert. . . . Albert's dearest name is immortalized with this *great* conception, *his* own, and my *own* dear country *showed* she was *worthy* of it."

The Ode composed by Tennyson for the opening of the Exhibition of 1862 reflected more accurately the mood which had prevailed in 1851:

> O ye, the wise who think, the wise who reign,
> From growing commerce loose her latest chain,
> And let the fair white-wing'd peacemaker fly
> To happy havens under all the sky,
> And mix the seasons and the golden hours;
> Till each man find his own in all men's good,
> And all men work in noble brotherhood,
> Breaking their mailed fleets and armed towers,
> And ruling by obeying Nature's powers,
> And gathering all the fruits of earth
> And crown'd with all her flowers.

History is strangely ironical. The great Peace Exhibition of 1851 was in fact followed by two decades of war: the war in the Crimea; the Sepoy war in India; the war of Italian Independence; the Civil War in America; the disastrous adventure in Mexico; the war of the Danish Duchies; the Seven Weeks' War between Prussia and Austria; the Franco-German War of 1871. Nor did the "wise who reign from growing commerce loose her latest chain." On the contrary, the period of war was followed by the era of high protection. So faded the dream of the Manchester School.

To return to the political scene in England. Each year that passed provided further justification for the Queen's misgivings as to Russell's capacity for his place. But his position was not an easy one, and even a stronger man might have failed to surmount the difficulties which beset him. He had no independent majority behind him; he was maintained in office partly by the support of the Peelites, partly by the lack of cohesion in the Opposition. A weak Opposition never makes for a strong Government. Lord John was Prime Minister on sufferance; and his position, never easy, was rendered more difficult, on the one hand by his rash incursions into ecclesiastical affairs, and on the other by his failure to control his impetuous and strong-willed colleague at the Foreign Office.

The appointment of Dr. Hampden, an eminent Liberal theologian, to the see of Hereford in 1847, aroused a storm of protest both from Evangelicals and Tractarians. The successful appeal of Mr. Gorham, a clergyman who had been refused institution by Bishop Philpotts of Exeter, further excited the indignation of High Churchmen. The Gorham judgment was, however, a trivial matter compared with the "insolent and insidious" (the phrase is Russell's) conduct of Pope Pius IX. In September 1850 the Pope

By kind permission of the Proprietors of "Punch"

THERE'S ALWAYS SOMETHING

"I'm very sorry, Palmerston, that you cannot agree with your fellow servants; but as I don't feel inclined to part with John, you must go, of course."

issued a Bill dividing England into twelve territorial dioceses with Father Wiseman, now raised to the Cardinalate and designated Archbishop of Westminster, at their head. In 1851 Parliament on Russell's initiative passed the *Ecclesiastical Titles Bill*, declaring the Papal Bull null and void, and imposing heavy penalties on all who attempted to give effect to it. The Act provided a temporary safety-valve for the excited feelings of English Protestants; but it remained a dead letter, and in 1871 was unobtrusively repealed.

Early in the same session a motion for assimilating the county to the borough franchise was carried against the Government, and Lord John, whose position had been rendered still more precarious by Peel's death, resigned (February 22). The Queen then sent for Lord Stanley, but Stanley, having vainly endeavoured to induce Mr. Gladstone to join him, found himself unable to form a Ministry. But the Peelites equally refused to join Russell. So the latter, after a week's interregnum, announced (March 3) that in obedience to the Queen, acting on the advice of the Duke of Wellington, to whom in her perplexity she had turned, he had resumed office.

The agony was not, however, unduly prolonged. The troubles with Lord Palmerston (to be discussed in a later chapter) came to a head in connection with Louis Napoleon's *coup d'état* in December 1851. Palmerston, at the Queen's instigation, was dismissed, but within two months he administered his "tit for tat" to his late colleagues. The Russell Ministry were defeated on their *Militia Bill* (February 20, 1852), and Lord John insisted on resignation. Lord Stanley, as we shall see later, then came in, but held office only until December 1852. Just a month earlier the nation had paid its last tribute of affection and respect to the greatest Englishman of his generation. On November 18 the Duke of Wellington, who had died in the previous September, was buried in St. Paul's Cathedral:

> Our greatest yet with least pretence,
> Great in council and great in war,
> Foremost captain of his time,
> Rich in saving common-sense,
> And, as the greatest only are,
> In his simplicity sublime.

Did Tennyson exaggerate? "Great in war" unquestionably; was the Duke also "great in council"? For party leadership, under the conditions of Parliamentary Democracy, he was manifestly unfitted. He was a good judge of men, but had no love for them. An acute critic has observed that "he had an intellectual contempt for his social equals, and a social contempt for his intellectual equals." It is true. Nevertheless, he had outstanding virtues; in him appeared

> The constant service of the antique world.

He was devotedly loyal to his Sovereign and to his country, and was honestly convinced that he alone stood between them and the revolutionary anarchy which threatened both with ruin. Whether, even in old age, he abandoned that conviction is uncertain, but at any rate he lived long enough to become the idol of a people who thirty years earlier had broken the windows of his palace in Piccadilly. So it was amid "an Empire's lamentation," "to the noise of the mourning of a mighty nation," that the Iron Duke passed to his rest.

By kind permission of the Proprietors of "Punch"

THE NEW SERVANTS

MISTRESS—"Never mind! I have no objection to your taking the regular holidays, but you mustn't be wanting always to 'go out,' for it disturbs the house dreadfully."

CHAPTER V

THE COALITION AND THE CRIMEAN WAR

DEMOCRACY is commonly supposed to make for instability in government. Perhaps; but Ministries have exhibited more stability since the shooting of Niagara than during the middle-class régime (1832–67). In the eight years between 1851 and 1859 there were no fewer than five different Ministries in office, each of which was divided from the rest by nothing more than personal considerations. Party cohesion is indeed unobtainable except when Parties are divided on big issues. In the middle years of Queen Victoria's reign there were no such issues to divide them. It was pre-eminently a case of men, not measures.

But who was to succeed Lord Derby in 1852? The Conservatives having agreed to bury Protection, there was nothing to prevent their reunion with the Peelites; but neither was there anything of principle to divide the Peelites from the Whigs, and on personal grounds the Peelites disliked Russell, and even Palmerston, less than they disliked Disraeli.

The Queen parted from Lord Derby without regret, and resented his suggestion that she should seek the advice of Lord Lansdowne as to his successor. It was, she maintained, no business of an outgoing Minister to advise on that matter. The responsibility was the Queen's, and hers alone. She did in fact send for Lord Lansdowne and Lord Aberdeen together: but the former was too ill to obey the summons, and she commissioned Lord Aberdeen to form a Government. To her great satisfaction he accepted the task.

Lord Aberdeen[1] was nearing seventy when he became for the first time Prime Minister. He was a man of the highest character, of fine culture, and of ripe experience. He had been sent as Ambassador Extraordinary to Vienna in 1813, and in 1814 had represented Great Britain at the fateful Congress at Chatillon. He served as Foreign Secretary under the Duke of Wellington (1828–30), and again under Peel from 1841 to 1846. When the Peel Ministry fell, the Queen parted with the Foreign Minister with hardly less regret than with Peel himself. She spoke of them as her "two devoted friends" and deplored "the irreparable loss" she had sustained by their resignation. "Never during the five years that they were with me did they *ever* recommend a *person* or a thing that was not for my or the country's best." No wonder, then, that the Queen rejoiced at "our excellent Aberdeen's" success in forming "so brilliant and strong a Cabinet" in December 1852. "To have my faithful friend Aberdeen as Prime Minister is a great happiness and comfort."

Brilliant in personnel the new Cabinet unquestionably was; it would have been stronger had it been less brilliant. The strongest Cabinets are those in which, as in Pitt's, in Peel's, in Gladstone's and Disraeli's, the Prime Minister is *primus* without *pares*. That was by no means the case in Lord Aberdeen's. The main difficulty in its formation was not with Palmerston, who, with a meekness that portended trouble, accepted the Home Office, but with Lord John Russell, who, greatly concerned about his own "honour," was restless, petulant and undecided: he "would and he

[1] Gordon George Hamilton, fourth Earl of Aberdeen, b. 1784; ed. Harrow and Cambridge; Scottish Representative Peer (1806–14); Viscount Gordon (U.K. peerage) (1814); Foreign Secretary (1828–30); Secretary War and Colonies (1834–5 and 1841–6); P.M. (1852–5); d. 1860.

wouldn't," but was eventually persuaded to take the Foreign Office with the leadership of the House of Commons. After a few weeks, however, he resigned the Foreign Office, but, with questionable constitutional propriety, retained the leadership of the House as a Cabinet Minister without portfolio. The Queen regarded this as a *dangerous precedent*, and complained that "so important an innovation in the construction of the executive Government should have been practically decided upon by an arrangement intended to meet personal wants under peculiar and accidental circumstances, leaving the Queen the embarrassing alternative only, either to forgo the exercise of her own prerogative, or to damage by her own act the *formation* or *stability* of the new Government, both of paramount importance to the welfare of the country." The Queen's complaint was justified, but in June the position was regularized when Russell succeeded Lord Granville as President of the Council. The latter goodnaturedly descended to the Presidency of the Board of Trade.

The rest of Lord Aberdeen's colleagues were all men of distinction. Lord Clarendon succeeded Russell at the Foreign Office, and, though not personally acceptable to the Queen, proved himself one of the best Foreign Secretaries of the reign. The Duke of Newcastle was Secretary for War and the Colonies until, in 1854, the two Departments were separated, when Sir George Grey went to the Colonial Office. Sir James Graham was at the Admiralty; Sir Charles Wood at the India Office; Mr. Sidney Herbert, Secretary at War; Sir William Molesworth (the first "radical" to be admitted to the Cabinet), First Commissioner of Works; the Duke of Argyll, Privy Seal; and Lord Lansdowne was in the Cabinet without office. Mr. Gladstone as Chancellor of the Exchequer conferred still further lustre on the most distinguished and perhaps the weakest Cabinet of the reign.

Yet the Duke of Argyll has put it on record that none of the Cabinets in which he sat, worked together more harmoniously and with less individual friction.[1]

The explanation of the paradox may in this case be found in that combination of personal amiability and political ineptitude so characteristic of the Prime Minister. Those qualities were, however, responsible for something even more serious than the weakness of the Cabinet.

Hardly had the new Ministers settled into their offices when the Near Eastern volcano burst into one of its periodical eruptions. The causes of the Crimean War have been endlessly discussed, but that Louis Napoleon was the immediate firebrand is indisputable. In 1850 he took up with great zeal the cause of the Roman Catholics in the Near East, insisting more particularly on the claims of the Latin monks to the guardianship of the Holy places in Palestine. The Greek Church hotly resisted those claims. This quarrel may have given occasion for the Crimean War. The causes of the war are to be found in the long-standing rivalry between the Russians and the Ottoman Turks. Not the Emperor Napoleon but the Czar Nicholas is now regarded as the principal villain of the piece.

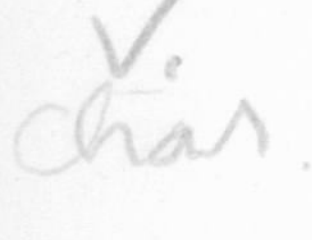

On his visit to England in 1844 the Czar had, however, fascinated both Lord Aberdeen and the Sovereign. The Queen quickly recovered from her infatuation; Lord Aberdeen did not. Palmerston had never yielded to it. On the contrary, ever since the conclusion of the Treaty of Unkiar-Skelessi, mistrust of Russian ambition had been the keynote of Palmerston's policy. By that treaty Russia established a virtual protectorate over European Turkey. Palmerston was determined to tear it up, and torn up it was by the Treaties of London (1840 and 1841).

But with the Crimean War this narrative cannot concern

[1] *Autobiography*, I, 388.

itself except in so far as the conduct of it throws light upon the relations between the Queen and her Ministers. Now as always the idea of war was abhorrent to the Queen. It was equally abhorrent to Lord Aberdeen. But between Queen and Minister there was a difference. Once the country was actually involved in war, the Queen was determined that it should be prosecuted to a successful issue. Aberdeen was as incompetent in the conduct of the war itself as he was fumbling in his pre-war diplomacy.

Could more skilful and resolute leadership have averted war? Kinglake ascribed the responsibility for its outbreak to Napoleon III: but Napoleon was his successful rival in an affair of the heart, and Kinglake was prejudiced. Queen Victoria imputed all the blame to the "selfishness and ambition of *one* man and his servants." Yet that man—the Czar Nicholas—not merely diagnosed the situation more accurately than any other statesman in Europe, but prescribed a remedy which, if applied, might have averted the Crimean War, and presumably have solved the problem of the Near East.

The sick man at Constantinople was, in his view, at the point of dissolution. England and Russia ought to act as the executors of his estate. Not only as executors but beneficiaries. Let England secure her route to India by annexing Egypt, Cyprus, and perhaps Crete: and give Russia a free hand in the Balkans, which would no longer be important to England. That was, in rough, the proposal made by Nicholas when he visited England in 1844, and repeated more specifically in his interviews with the British Ambassador at Petersburg in 1853.

The proposals shocked Aberdeen's sense of diplomatic decency and were summarily rejected. In retrospect Lord Salisbury could (in 1897) lament a lost opportunity. Is it certain that in 1853 he would have been any more ready than Aberdeen to adopt so crude a suggestion? Yet, notwithstanding his rejection of the Czar's proposals, Aberdeen still protested to the Queen his confidence that a peaceful solution of the matter would be found; and even on June 22, 1853, the Queen could write to King Leopold: "I feel convinced that *war will be avoided*, but I don't see *how* exactly."

Nor did anyone else. In 1854 the war broke out. The Queen, as already mentioned, held the Czar Nicholas to be solely responsible and did not shrink from upbraiding those Powers which refused to join in inflicting upon him the punishment he deserved. In particular, she dealt faithfully with King Frederick William IV of Prussia. The letters which in 1854 the Queen addressed to him must surely be unique in the correspondence of friendly sovereigns. In the first she writes on March 17:

DEAR SIR AND BROTHER,—

General Count von der Gröben has brought me the official letter of your Majesty as well as the confidential one. . . . He will be able to tell you orally what I can express only imperfectly in writing, how deep my pain is, after our going so far, faithfully, hand in hand, to see you, at this weighty moment, separating yourself from us. My pain is still further increased by the fact that I cannot even conceive the grounds which move your Majesty to take this step. . . .

The dreadful and incalculable consequences of a War weigh upon my heart not less than on your Majesty's. I also know that the Emperor of Russia does not wish for it. He, none the less, demands from the Porte things which all the Powers of Europe—among them yourself—have solemnly declared to be incompatible with the independence of the Porte and the European balance of power. In view of this declaration and of the presence of the Russian Army of invasion in the Principalities, the Powers could not but be ready to confirm their word by action. . . . If now your Majesty informs me that "*now you mean to persist in complete neutrality*, and if on this occasion your refer us to your Nation . . ." I do not understand you. Certainly I should understand this language if I heard it from the Kings of Hanover or of Saxony. But I have, hitherto, looked upon Prussia as one of the Great Powers which, since the peace of 1815, have been guarantors of treaties, guardians of civilization, defenders of the right, and real arbiters of the Nations, and for my part I have felt the divine responsibility of this sacred office, without undervaluing at the same time the heavy obligation, not unconnected with danger, which it imposes on me. If you, dear Sir and Brother, abdicate these obligations, you have also abdicated that position for Prussia. And should such an example find imitators, then the civilization of Europe would be delivered up to the play of winds; right will then no longer find a champion, the oppressed will find no longer an umpire. . . .

To come to a close. You suppose that War may already have been declared; you express, however, at the same time, the hope that it may not already have actually broken out. I cannot unfortunately hold out any hope that the sentence will be followed by any stay of execution. Shakespeare's words,

> Beware
> Of entrance to a quarrel; but, being in,
> Bear it that the opposer may beware of thee,

are deeply engraved on the hearts of all Englishmen. Sad that they are to find an application at this crisis in a nation with whom previously nothing prevailed but friendship and affection! And how much more melancholy must be the present emotions of your Majesty's heart and mind to see such words applied to a beloved brother-in-law, whom yet—however much you love him—your conscience cannot absolve from the crime of having brought upon the world wilfully and frivolously such awful misery! . . .

This remarkable and characteristic letter concludes with a prayer not less sincere, doubtless, than the rest of it: "May the Almighty take you under His protection"! The Queen evidently thought the Prussian King to be sorely in need of it.

The King replied apologetically: "May your Majesty believe my Royal Word. I was, I am, I remain the truest and most faithful friend of Great Britain. . . . I cannot and will not side with Russia because Russia's arrogance and wickedness have caused this *horrible* trouble, and because duty and conscience and tradition forbid me to draw the sword against Old England." Nevertheless, he persists in neutrality. By June the King has become the Queen's "Dearest Sir and Brother," but increased affection has not diminished the Queen's bluntness, and she tells him frankly that if he is so anxious for the restoration of peace he can best expedite it by "vigorous co-operation" just as he might "by vigorous co-operation" have helped to prevent the outbreak of war.

With statesmen at home, the Queen dealt at least as faithfully as with foreign sovereigns. No Minister, however personally acceptable to her, could retain her confidence if he displayed lack of vigour or political courage when England was at war. Her own attitude was unambiguous. War she detested, but once convinced that it was inevitable, her brave heart knew no shrinking, her tireless vigilance neglected no detail that could contribute to its speedy and successful termination. One day (February 24, 1854) she writes to Lord Aberdeen to urge upon his attention a matter of "paramount importance"—the immediate augmentation of the army, the provision of adequate reserves, etc. Another day she writes to the Duke of Newcastle, then Secretary for War, to get assurance as to the "*effective* state" of the home defences:

"What store of muskets are there *here*? . . . What is the force of artillery left in the country in men and horses? . . . What is the Naval Force at home? How much serviceable ammunition is there, both of artillery and small arms, in the country?"

A third letter goes to Lord John Russell to express "her sense of the *imperative importance* of the Cabinet being *united* and of one mind at this moment, and not to let it *appear* that there are differences of opinion within it. The knowledge that there are such is a source of great *anxiety* to the Queen."

Not less characteristic was the Queen's protest against the proposal to proclaim a "Day of Humiliation." John Bright described Queen Victoria as the most absolutely truthful person he had ever known. Her truthfulness would not allow her to sanction a "Day of Humiliation."

". . . Really to say (as we probably should) that the *great sinfulness of the nation* has brought about this War when it is the selfishness and ambition of *one* man and his servants who have brought this about, while our conduct has been throughout actuated by unselfishness and honesty, would be too manifestly repulsive to the feelings of everyone and would be a mere act of hypocrisy. Let there be a prayer expressive of our great thankfulness for the benefits we have enjoyed, and for the immense prosperity of this country, and entreating God's help and protection in the coming struggle. In this the Queen would join heart and soul. If there is to be a day set apart, let it be for prayer in this sense. . . ."

Similarly, during the Indian Mutiny, the Queen willingly sanctioned a "day of prayer and intercession for our suffering countrymen," though she resented the idea of "fast and humiliation."

Constant anxiety about her soldiers and sailors, ceaseless efforts to mitigate their sufferings, tender sympathy for the relations of those who fell in battle—all this was natural to the Queen, but to profess a "humiliation" which she did not feel—never! The great work done by Miss Florence Nightingale—the "lady of the lamp"—made a special appeal to the Queen, as the following characteristic letter shows:

WINDSOR CASTLE,
Jan. 1856.

DEAR MISS NIGHTINGALE,—

You are, I know, well aware of the high sense I entertain of the Christian devotion which you have displayed during this great and bloody war, and I need hardly repeat to you how warm my admiration is for your services, which are fully equal to those of my dear and brave soldiers, whose sufferings you have had the privilege of alleviating in so merciful a manner; I am, however, anxious of marking my feelings in a manner which I trust will be agreeable to you, and, therefore, send you with this letter a brooch, the form and emblems of which commemorate your great and blessed work, and which, I hope, you will wear as a mark of the high approbation of your Sovereign. It will be a very great satisfaction to me, when you return at last to these shores, to make the acquaintance of one who has set so bright an example to our sex. And with every prayer for the preservation of your valuable health, believe me, always yours sincerely,

VICTORIA R.

With the conduct of her Ministers she was less well satisfied. She thought them lukewarm in the prosecution of the war, and did not conceal her opinion. They thought her unnecessarily fussy. She was elated by the victories of the Alma, of Inkerman and Balaclava in the autumn of 1854, but the "sad privations and constant sickness" of the army during the terrible winter of 1854–5 preyed greatly on her mind.

Nor was she alone in her anxiety.

The country at large was deeply concerned to learn through *The Times* of the breakdown of the transport and commissariat arrangements, and, worst of all, of the shocking conditions in the hospital at Scutari. There were 13,000 men in hospital by the end of February, and the mortality was 50 per cent.

The prevailing anxiety and discontent compelled the Government to summon Parliament in December, and Mr. J. A. Roebuck promptly gave notice of a motion for the appointment of a Select Committee "to enquire into the condition of our army before Sebastopol and into the conduct of those departments of the Government whose duty it has been to minister to the wants of that army." On January 29 the motion was carried by an overwhelming majority. Lord Aberdeen at once resigned. The Queen parted from him with genuine regret and sought to solace him with the Garter. But his career was ended and he died in 1860. Aberdeen has been described as "the British Aristides," and a noble panegyric was pronounced on him by Mr. Gladstone. "All the qualities and parts," he wrote, "in which he was great were those that are the very foundation-stones of our being; as foundation-stones they are deep, and as being deep they are withdrawn from view; but time is their witness and their friend, and in the final distribution of posthumous fame Lord Aberdeen has nothing to forfeit, he has only to receive." Mr. Gladstone was lamenting the loss of a dear friend, and a good man. Of Lord Aberdeen as statesman posterity has but confirmed the judgment of contemporaries. Had his lot been cast in tranquil days, History might have acclaimed him as a successful Prime Minister; but he was quite unfitted to ride a whirlwind or direct a storm.

CHAPTER VI

LORD PALMERSTON, THE LAST OF THE WHIGS

ON Lord Aberdeen's resignation the Queen sent for Lord Derby; but despite Disraeli's magnanimous offer to surrender the lead of the House to Palmerston and the Exchequer to Gladstone, Lord Derby, after much negotiation, relinquished his attempt to form a Government.

The Queen then, reluctantly, sent for Lord John Russell. But he discovered, to his surprise and chagrin, that none of his late colleagues, Whigs or Peelites, with the sole exception of Palmerston, would serve under him. His resignation, already recorded, on the eve of the Roebuck debate, was generally condemned as disloyal and pusillanimous. "To escape punishment he ran away from duty." Such was Mr. Gladstone's verdict. The Queen bluntly dubbed him a "deserter." Palmerston told him to his face that he had held on to office, abetting a policy of which he disapproved, until he was frightened into resignation by Roebuck's notice of motion.

Having exhausted the alternatives, the Queen at last sent for Lord Palmerston, who thus became Prime Minister for the first time at the age of 71.[1] His Cabinet was virtually the

[1] Temple, Henry John, third Viscount Palmerston, b. 1784; ed. Harrow and Cambridge; Tory M.P. for Newport, I.W. (1807); Lord of the Admiralty (1808); Secretary-at-War (1809–28); M.P. for Cambridge University (1811–31); South Hants (1832); Tiverton (1835–65); Foreign Secretary (1830–41 and 1846–51); Home Secretary (1852–5); P.M. (1855–8 and 1859–65); d. 1865.

Aberdeen Cabinet without Russell, Newcastle, who as War Secretary was held specially responsible for the maladministration of the Army, and Aberdeen himself. Within a fortnight, however, Palmerston lost Mr. Gladstone, Sir James Graham and Mr. Sidney Herbert, who resigned on learning that with the assent of the Government the Roebuck enquiry was to be carried through. Mr. Roebuck became Chairman of the "Sebastopol Committee," which reported before the end of June. The Chairman's draft Report was almost entirely superseded in favour of one by Lord Seymour, afterwards Duke of Somerset. It lost most of its significance, however, because the Government (Aberdeen's) which it severely censured, had already fallen, and still more because the war itself was now being conducted to a successful and speedy termination.

The Czar Nicholas succumbed to an attack of influenza on March 2, 1855; Lord Raglan, who, in face of every discouragement, had held on with unfaltering courage and grim tenacity to the task entrusted to him, fell a victim to cholera on June 28; on September 8 the Allies entered Sebastopol. The Emperor Napoleon was tired of the War, and on March 30, 1856, the definitive Peace was signed at Paris.

The war had brought considerable prestige to France and her Emperor; still more to Sardinia, who had come in as the ally of the Western Powers in 1855; but to England very little. The claim of Russia to a protectorate over the Balkan States was repudiated and her preponderance in the Black Sea was ended—but only until 1871, when it was, with Bismarck's connivance if not at his suggestion, effectively reasserted. The Danubian Principalities were virtually emancipated from the rule of the Turks and presently united in the Kingdom of Roumania. The Turk, relieved of the fear of Russian advance by the intervention of the Western Powers, was bidden to put his house in order. Of course he neglected to do so, with the result that twelve years later the whole Eastern Question was reopened and a repetition of the Crimean War was narrowly averted by the promptitude and firmness of the Queen and Lord Beaconsfield. Whether a similar policy firmly applied to the parallel situation of 1853 might not have met with equal success is one of those open questions which can never be resolved. What is certain is that, with all his virtues, Lord Aberdeen was not the man to apply it, and that not until his supersession by Lord Palmerston was the war, into which the Coalition Ministry had drifted, conducted with vigour to a successful end.

Hardly had the war ended before Napoleon's conduct began to cause grave disquietude in England. Palmerston had always been mistrustful of the Emperor. "In our alliance with France we are riding a runaway horse and must always be on our guard." Such was the view he frequently expressed. He even envisaged a union between France and Russia to effect "some great scheme of mutual ambition." But the first of Napoleon's many projects was a partition of North Africa: Morocco for France, Tunis for Sardinia, and for England Egypt, with the control of the proposed canal through the Isthmus of Suez. Napoleon's suggestion shocked Palmerston as much as the Czar's had shocked Aberdeen. Nor was it intrinsically tempting to statesmen who were still dominated by the ideas of the Manchester School. "We want to trade with Egypt, and to travel through Egypt, but we do not want the burden of governing Egypt." Such was the fashionable creed of the day.

Still less did we want to govern Persia; but in November 1856 the Indian Government found itself involved in war with Persia, on account of the latter's refusal to withdraw from Herat, then regarded as the "Gate of India." The war lasted only a few months and was ended by a Treaty signed in Paris in March 1857. Persia renounced all claims to Herat or any other part of Afghanistan; but Palmerston did not regard the matter lightly. "We are beginning," he said, "to repel the first opening of trenches against India by Russia."

He had other troubles on his hands. In the autumn of 1856 a dispute broke out with China about the coasting schooner or lorcha *Arrow*. The rights of the matter were hotly disputed, not only in China, but at Westminster, and in the House of Commons a motion condemning the "high-handed action" of the Government was carried by a majority of 16. Cobden, who proposed the motion, took into the Lobby, not Russell, Gladstone, and Graham only, but Disraeli.

Palmerston at once appealed to the country for a vote of confidence, and came back with a clear majority of over 50. Cobden lost his seat: his allies, John Bright and Milner Gibson, were defeated at Manchester; in fine, the "Pacifists" were smitten hip and thigh. Palmerston's majority was purely a personal one. Unfortunately he was too quick to interpret it in that sense; he played the dictator, and within a twelvemonth the dictator was dethroned. In the meantime he had to deal with one of the most serious crises in the recent history of the Empire.

That crisis showed Palmerston at his worst; it showed Queen Victoria at her best. The Queen's confidence in Palmerston, never robust, was still further shaken by the levity with which he treated the news of the Sepoy mutiny in India. The levity was more apparent than real, but was hardly on that account the more excusable. The truth is that, despite his seventy years, despite nearly half a century of parliamentary experience and over forty years of official life, Palmerston was still incurably youthful.

He had begun political and official life as a Tory; but his Toryism was of the Canning rather than the Eldon type. Even before Canning's death (1827) he was already beginning to talk of the "stupid old Tory party," and in 1830 he accepted office as Foreign Secretary in the "Reform" Ministry of Earl Grey. At the Foreign Office he remained continuously (save for four months in the winter of 1834–5) for eleven years; he served in the same office again for five years under Russell (1845–51), and was, as Prime Minister, largely responsible for the control of English policy abroad (except for fifteen months in 1858–9) from 1855 until his death in 1865. For a whole generation, therefore, Palmerston stood to foreigners for England; and both were regarded with mixed feelings at continental courts. The autocrats at Vienna, Berlin and St. Petersburg mistrusted the disciple of Canning. Palmerston mistrusted Napoleon III. Like his master, he preferred "to read for Europe England" and went on his own way heedless of the opinion of other people. An intense believer in his own country, he knew more about other countries than any other Englishman of his time. He had assiduously prepared himself for his life's work by foreign travel, and was a fluent linguist. He has some claim to be regarded as the creator of Belgium, he had a share in the making of Modern Greece, while in Italy his memory is still honoured as a champion of Italian independence. He was indeed no enemy to the Hapsburg Empire, so long as it refrained from the oppression of subject peoples; but to Kossuth he showed more friendliness than was prudent in a Foreign Secretary, and made no secret of his sympathy with the Italians in their efforts to drive the Austrians out of Lombardy and Venetia. He was convinced that the Italian Provinces were to the Austrian Empire a source not of strength but of weakness: "the heel of Achilles and not the shield of Ajax"; "the Alps," he said, "are her natural barrier and her best defence." "North of the Alps (he wrote to Ponsonby at Vienna) we wish her all the prosperity and success in the world."

As regards the Near East, he was profoundly mistrustful of Russia's designs on the Ottoman Empire. He tore up the Treaty of Unkiar-Skelessi in 1833, and by the Treaties of London (1840–1) and Paris (1856) he finally headed off Russia from Constantinople. His colleagues in the Melbourne Government were alarmed lest he should involve us in war with France in 1840; but, although he instructed Bulwer, the British ambassador in Paris, to tell M. Thiers "in the most friendly and inoffensive manner possible that if France throws down the gauntlet we shall not refuse to pick it up," he had no fear that that peace would be broken, being convinced "that Louis Philippe was not the man to run amuck without any adequate motive." The event proved that Palmerston had gauged the situation to a nicety.

His immense popularity in his own country was due in large measure to the prevailing belief that he was not merely a full-blooded patriot, but a "sportsman" who did not take life or politics too seriously. As a fact he took them much more seriously than he allowed people to suppose.

With the Queen Palmerston's relations were from first to last uneasy. He had a great respect for her abilities; directly she came to the throne he said that "any ministers who had to deal with her would soon find that she was no ordinary person." But he was prone to treat her somewhat as the elderly family solicitor used to treat his young lady clients in unenfranchised days: "My dear young lady, don't trouble your pretty head by reading the long documents I send you: you won't understand them if you do; you can trust me; just sign and return them."

The Queen deeply resented this attitude, and repeatedly complained of it both to Lord John Russell, as Prime

Minister, and to Palmerston himself. The following letter is characteristic of many:

OSBORNE,
17 *April*, 1848.

The Queen not having heard anything from Lord Palmerston respecting foreign affairs for so long a time, and as he must be in constant communication with the Foreign Ministers in these most eventful and anxious times, writes to urge Lord Palmerston to keep her informed of what he hears, and of the views of the Government on the important questions before us. She now only gets the drafts when they are gone. The acceptance of the mediation between Denmark and Holstein is too important an event not to have been first submitted to the Queen.

Palmerston's reply was not calculated to soothe the Queen's ruffled feelings, and did not, in reality, meet her point at all:

CARLTON GARDENS,
18 *April*, 1848.

Viscount Palmerston presents his humble duty to your Majesty, and regrets much that he has not lately had an opportunity of giving your Majesty verbally such explanations as your Majesty might wish to receive with respect to the progress of foreign affairs, but . . . although events of the greatest importance have been passing in rapid succession in almost every part of Europe, the position of your Majesty's Government has been one rather of observation than of action, it being desirable that England should keep herself as free as possible from unnecessary engagements and entanglements, in order that your Majesty may be at liberty to take such decisions as the state of things may from time to time appear to render most advisable.

On September 19 of the same year the Queen wrote to Lord John that the time had come when she "must speak quite openly to him about Lord Palmerston." "That I felt really," she proceeds, "I could hardly go on with him, that I had no confidence in him, and that it made me seriously anxious and uneasy for the welfare of the country and for the peace of Europe."

Palmerston, however, though professing contrition to his chief, did not materially mend his ways, and at last (August 12, 1850) the Queen sent to him, through the Prime Minister, the memorandum which, though frequently quoted, is too important to be omitted:

OSBORNE,
12 *August*, 1850.

With reference to the conversation about Lord Palmerston which the Queen had with Lord John Russell the other day, and Lord Palmerston's disavowal that he ever intended any disrespect to her by the various neglects of which she had so long and so often to complain, she thinks it right, in order *to prevent any mistake* for the *future*, shortly to explain *what it is she expects from her Foreign Secretary*. She requires: (1) That he will distinctly state what he proposes in a given case, in order that the Queen may know as distinctly to what she has given her Royal sanction. (2) Having *once given* her sanction to a measure, that it be not arbitrarily altered or modified by the Minister; such an act she must consider as failing in sincerity towards the Crown, and justly to be visited by the exercise of her Constitutional right of dismissing that Minister. She expects to be kept informed of what passes between him and the Foreign Ministers before important decisions are taken, based upon that intercourse; to receive the Foreign Despatches in good time, and to have the drafts for her approval sent to her in sufficient time to make herself acquainted with their contents before they must be sent off. The Queen thinks it best that Lord John Russell should show this letter to Lord Palmerston.

Lord Palmerston assured the Prime Minister that he "would not fail to attend to the directions which the memorandum contained." Before the end of 1851, however, he was in deeper disgrace than ever. In October 1851 Louis Kossuth, one of the leaders of the Hungarian insurrection of 1848, visited England. It was announced that he was to be received by the Foreign Secretary. The Queen was greatly agitated by this news; Lord John insisted that the proposed interview would be "improper and unnecessary," and virtually interdicted it. Palmerston angrily retorted: "I do not choose to be dictated to as to whom I may or may not receive in my own house." The Cabinet supported the Premier and Palmerston gave way; but a few weeks later he received a deputation of Radicals who presented an address in which the Emperors of Russia and Austria were referred to as "odious and detestable assassins." So gross a breach of international good manners caused further and deep annoyance to the Queen: Lord John did not attempt to justify his colleague, yet hesitated to dismiss him.

There was worse to come. On December 3 news reached London that Louis Napoleon had carried out a successful *coup d'état*, and had virtually overthrown the Republic of which he was President, and destroyed the Constitution he had sworn to defend. The Queen bade her Ministers observe strict neutrality, and orders in that sense were sent to Lord Normanby, the British ambassador in Paris. Normanby, however, learnt from the French Government that Palmerston had privately expressed to Count Waleski, the French ambassador in London, his approval of the *coup d'état*. Normanby's position in Paris was thereby rendered exceedingly embarrassing, the more so as Louis Napoleon had previously complained to Lord Malmesbury that he, Lord Normanby, was corresponding to his detriment with Prince Albert. Even if he were, the ambassador's indiscretion could not excuse Lord Palmerston's. Nor was the Queen or the Premier disposed to condone it. On December 19 Palmerston was dismissed. The Duke of Argyll, writing to Lord Aberdeen,[1] opined that the Waleski incident supplied "no sufficient ground for such an abrupt dismissal," and assumed (correctly, as we now know), that "it was but the drop which made the cup o'erflow." The Queen, writing to King Leopold, expressed her delight in terms even less restrained than usual:

23 *December*, 1851.

MY DEAREST UNCLE,—

I have the greatest pleasure in announcing to you a piece of news which I know will give you as much satisfaction and relief as it does to us, and will do to the *whole* of the world. *Lord Palmerston is no longer Foreign Secretary*. . . . He had become of late really quite reckless. . . .

Palmerston's dismissal caused immense satisfaction at Vienna and Berlin. Prince Felix Schwarzenberg, the Austrian Chancellor, gave a ball in honour of the event; the Prussian view was expressed in a once famous couplet:

Hat der Teufel einen Sohn,
So ist er sicher Palmerston.

Lord John proposed that Lord Granville should succeed Palmerston at the Foreign Office; the Queen cordially approved; but the Cabinet overruled the Prime Minister and insisted that the post should first be offered to Lord Clarendon. To this unusual and unconstitutional procedure

[1] *Autobiography*, I, 348.

the Queen very properly demurred, and "protested against the Cabinet's taking upon itself the appointment of its own members, which rested entirely with the Prime Minister and the Sovereign under whose approval the former constructed his Government." The reproof was well deserved, but Lord John was never a Prime Minister in the same sense as Pitt, Peel, Gladstone or Disraeli. Palmerston declined a derisive offer of the Lord-Lieutenancy of Ireland with an English peerage, but he treated the whole incident with characteristic good-humour, and, as already mentioned, he had not long to wait for his revenge. The Queen supposed that she had finally got rid of him, and that (as she wrote to King Leopold) " 'the veteran statesman'," as the newspapers, to our great amusement and, I am sure, to *his* infinite annoyance, call him, must rest upon his laurels."

The Queen was mistaken: so was Disraeli, who wrote: "There *was* a Pam." Palmerston had still eleven years of office ahead of him, and during nine of them he was the First Minister of the Crown. In Lord Aberdeen's Ministry he served, as we have seen, as Home Secretary, and on Aberdeen's resignation became Prime Minister.

His first business was to bring to a successful end the Crimean War. That done he had to deal with mutiny in India.

There is no doubt that among the causes of that outbreak one was the report sedulously circulated in the bazaars that Russia was beating England in the Crimea.

As early as October 1854, the Governor-General, Lord Dalhousie, had written to the Queen about the indirect influence of the Crimean War on India, which he described as "most sensibly apparent." "The notions entertained of Russia and the estimate formed of her powers by the natives of India are," he proceeded, "exaggerated in the extreme. Although our pride must wince on hearing it, it is an unquestionable fact that the general belief in India at this moment is that Russia gravely menaces the power of England, and will be more than a match for her in the end. This feeling cannot prudently be disregarded," even though India is "at present absolutely safe." On leaving India (February 1856) he wrote home: "We are perfectly secure so long as we are strong and are believed to be so." At the same time he protested strongly against the withdrawal of British regiments from India and insisted on the dangers involved in the increasing disproportion between British and native troops. His warnings were unheeded. Within fifteen months of his departure the Mutiny broke out.

During the anxious months that followed the Queen suffered, as her biographer has truly said, "acute mental torture," and her feelings are faithfully reflected in her constant correspondence with her Ministers, particularly with the Prime Minister, with Lord Panmure, Secretary for War, and with Lord Canning, who had just succeeded Dalhousie as Governor-General. The Queen suspected that the Cabinet failed to realize the gravity of the crisis, and she deplored the inadequacy and tardiness of the measures they were taking to meet it. She insisted that large reinforcements under good officers should be promptly sent out, and that the home establishment thus denuded should be kept up to strength. She repeatedly warned Palmerston that "the measures hitherto taken by the Government are not commensurate," and on September 2 wrote to King Leopold: "We are in sad anxiety about India, which engrosses all our attention. Troops cannot be raised fast or largely enough. And the horrors committed on the poor ladies—women and children . . . make one's blood run cold. . . . There is not a family hardly who is not in sorrow and anxiety about their children, and in all ranks." Fortunately, a considerable British Force was already on its way to China when the

Indian Mutiny broke out, and was promptly directed to India by Lord Canning, with the cordial assent of Lord Elgin, Plenipotentiary in China. But great as was the Queen's satisfaction at hearing this news, it hardly diminished her persistence. Palmerston with ill-timed jocularity had written to say that it was "fortunate for the Government that the Queen was not sitting on the Opposition benches in the House of Commons." But the Queen was far too anxious to perceive the sarcasm underlying his words.

In December the Queen opened Parliament in person, and by May 1858 the suppression of the Mutiny was so far completed as to justify the holding of a Public Thanksgiving (May 1), though it was not until April 1859 that the last embers of the insurrectionary fire had been stamped out.

Meanwhile Parliament had decided that the time had come when the Crown must assume direct and formal responsibility for the government of this great dependency.

But before this momentous change was effected, Lord Palmerston's Government had fallen on the Conspiracy to Murder Bill. This abortive measure was introduced in order to placate the French people and their Emperor. In January 1858 an anarchist named Orsini had attempted to murder the Emperor and Empress of the French. Orsini was an Italian, but the conspiracy had been hatched and the fatal bombs had been manufactured in England. Against England, and particularly against her flippant and provocative Prime Minister, bitter indignation was expressed in Paris. The French army demanded to be led against that "den of assassins"; "the infamous haunt in which machinations so infernal are planned ought," they urged, "to be destroyed for ever."

The whole incident was seriously mishandled by Palmerston, and when his Conspiracy to Murder Bill was introduced, he was defeated in the House of Commons. The

Queen was anxious, under the circumstances of the moment, to avoid a change of Ministry. Lord Derby, the obvious alternative to Palmerston, was strongly averse to taking office in a minority, but Palmerston persisted in his resignation, and Lord Derby came in. His Ministry was, however, defeated in the House of Commons (March 1859); Parliament was dissolved in April; the elections gave the Liberals a diminished but just sufficient majority (43), and on a vote of censure Lord Derby resigned (June 11).

The Queen thereupon sent for Lord Granville. He was personally acceptable to her and she wished to avoid the necessity of an invidious choice between "the two old men," both of whom had been Prime Minister, and neither of whom she liked. But, foreseeing difficulties, she personally appealed both to Lord Palmerston and Lord John to support Lord Granville. Palmerston genially consented; Russell curtly refused. Granville was compelled, therefore, to resign the commission entrusted to him by the Queen. Palmerston came in a second time as Prime Minister, and Russell joined him, but, to the intense annoyance of the Queen, insisted on the Foreign Office as the price of his adhesion. Gladstone, who had seceded from Palmerston's first Ministry after a fortnight of office, returned to the Exchequer, where he made financial history.

But the key-post in the Government was the Foreign Office. The Italian War of Independence Lord John might well have foreseen, and have wished to be in control of British policy during a time so critical for a cause to which he was devoted. But he could hardly have foreseen the American Civil War, and the complications arising therefrom; still less the war waged by Bismarck for the acquisition of Schleswig-Holstein. These were the matters on which attention was to be focussed.

Of the continental movements of the nineteenth century

none excited more sympathetic interest in England than the Italian *Risorgimento*—the progress of Italy towards independence and unity. From the time of the Peace Settlement of 1815 down to the year of Revolution (1848–9), the yoke of Austria had lain heavy on most of the many States into which Italy was divided. The petty Princes danced to the tune called by Metternich from Vienna. Metternich fell in 1848; Italy blazed out into insurrection; Venice offered an heroic resistance to the Austrians; Rome to the French; but by 1849 the *status quo ante* was everywhere restored. In 1852, however, Mr. Gladstone addressed to Lord Aberdeen the famous letters which revealed to the world the hideous misgovernment of the Bourbons in Southern Italy; in 1854 Sardinia sent her contingent to fight side by side with the English and French in the Crimea; and in 1856 Count Cavour took his place as Minister of Sardinia among the statesmen of Europe at the Conference of Paris. He there aroused the interest of Lord Clarendon in the Italian question; and still more to his purpose, that of Napoleon III. At the end of 1855 Count Cavour and his king, Victor Emmanuel, had visited the Queen, and though she was rather startled at first by "her royal brother's" manners and appearance, she formed a good impression of his sound sense and straightforwardness. Consequently, she cordially approved Lord Clarendon's championship of the Sardinian cause at the Paris Conference, as she had "the greatest respect for that noble little country" and its "honest, straightforward as well as courageous king."

By 1859 the wind had shifted. The French Emperor was preparing to fight Austria. Palmerston, as already mentioned, had always desired the withdrawal of Austria from Italy: Russell and Gladstone were ardently attached to the Italian cause. The Queen, however, spared no efforts to avert war; she was concerned for the vested rights of Austria, and mistrusted the designs of Napoleon. Not without reason. Having proclaimed his intention to "free Italy from the Alps to the Adriatic," Napoleon stopped short at the Mincio: left Venetia in the hands of Austria and consented to the union of Lombardy and the Central States of Italy with Sardinia only on condition that Savoy and Nice were added to France. In 1860 Garibaldi and his "Thousand" made themselves masters of Sicily and Naples, and Southern Italy was united with the Northern Kingdom under the sceptre of the House of Savoy. Only Venice and Rome remained outside the Italian Kingdom.

Continental Europe viewed these events with profound emotion. They constituted an attack on the Peace Settlement of 1815; they threatened the principle of "legitimacy" if not every vested interest. Garibaldi to Austria was a "brigand"; and Cavour was little better. Above all, what was to happen to the Pope, to Rome, to the Temporal Power? In England there was an acute difference of opinion between the Sovereign and her Ministers. The Queen's primary interest was the preservation of peace. When that was broken she wished England to observe strict neutrality. Palmerston, Gladstone and Russell—especially Russell—were ardently pro-Italian. Russell thought we might "have to interfere against the ruthless tyranny of Austria or the unchained ambition of France." His attitude "placed [the Queen] in a position of much difficulty, giving her great pain. She has been obliged to object to so many drafts sent to her from the Foreign Office on the Italian question, and yet no sooner is one withdrawn or altered than others are submitted exactly of the same purport or tendency, if even couched in different words" (August 24, 1859). The Queen more than once took the strong step of appealing to the Cabinet against the Foreign Secretary and the Prime Minister. Not wholly without success; for the Cabinet resented the independence and high-handedness of its chiefs. "Johnnie has had a lesson," wrote Lord Granville to a colleague, "that the Cabinet will prevent him and Pam from acting on important occasions without the advice of their colleagues." Lord Granville was, of all the members of that Cabinet, the one most trusted by the Queen, and more than once she wrote to him individually for information. The position was delicate: but rarely have the gifts of the courtier and the diplomatist been more conspicuously combined than in Granville's replies. He made it clear that Lord John "from a loose way of doing business" frequently overrode the decisions of the Cabinet, which was, on the Italian question, hopelessly divided. Thus without disloyalty to colleagues he contrived to give the Queen all the information she wanted.

A little later the Queen found it necessary to protest to the Prime Minister against the gross lack of respect shown to her by his impatient and irritable colleague. She forwarded to him a letter from Lord John beginning: "Lord John Russell unfortunately does not partake your Majesty's opinions in regard to Italy." He insinuated (to use the Queen's description) that she was indifferent to "the liberation of the Italian people from a foreign yoke," and that she was "no well-wisher of mankind and indifferent to its freedom and happiness." Lord John's letter was, to speak bluntly, exceedingly rude both in form and substance, and the Queen was entirely justified in demanding "that respect which is due from a Minister to his Sovereign" (February 10, 1860). Lord John expressed his regret and was pardoned. The value of the services then rendered by Great Britain to the Italian cause cannot, however, be overestimated and have never been forgotten. Without the support of England Garibaldi could not have crossed from Sicily to the mainland and made himself master of Naples. Without her support Cavour could not have united Southern Italy with the Northern Kingdom. At the critical moment (November 1860) a dispatch from Russell to the British Minister at Turin was published in Italy. "H.M. Government," he wrote, "can see no sufficient ground for the severe censure with which Austria, France, Russia and Prussia have visited the acts of the King of Sardinia. H.M. Government will turn their eyes rather to the gratifying prospect of a people building up the edifice of their liberties, and consolidating the work of their independence." That was, indeed, a defiance of the autocrats in the true Canningite manner. The Italians acclaimed the dispatch as worth "more than 100,000 men." Italy was "made," and England contributed not a little to its making.

In 1861 interest shifted to the other side of the Atlantic. The Southern States of the American Republic seceded from the Union, and on January 9 the first shot was fired in the Civil War. The sympathies of England were divided. Palmerston, Gladstone and some of their colleagues made no secret of their sympathy with the South. Cobden, John Bright and the Radicals generally, sympathized with the North; so did Lord Stanley; so also did the Court. Officially England proclaimed and observed strict neutrality, an attitude which compelled her to recognize the Southern Confederacy as belligerents. But the recognition, though logical, was deeply resented by the North; various incidents inflamed feelings between the two countries and brought them in November 1861 to the brink of war. Two Southern envoys, Slidell and Mason, having successfully run the Northern blockade, embarked at Havana on an English mail ship, the *Trent*. On November 8 a Federal ship of war intercepted the *Trent* and carried off the Southern envoys in custody to Boston. This flagrant violation of international law excited lively indignation in England. Earl Russell (as he had become in July) indited a dispatch demanding in the most peremptory language immediate redress, and threatening, in default, the withdrawal of our ambassador from Washington. The Prince Consort was alarmed by its tone, and though already a stricken man, carefully revised it in a sense which left open to President Lincoln a path of honourable retreat from a false position. The Queen endorsed her copy of the draft, "the last the beloved Prince ever wrote," and added that he was so ill he could hardly hold a pen. But he achieved his purpose. His wise suggestions were accepted by the Cabinet; the American Government grasped the olive branch; the danger of war was dispelled. This was the last but not the least of the services rendered by the Prince to his adopted country. He died on December 14. At long last the nation realized its loss and mourned with the widowed Queen. All classes of her people felt, as Disraeli said, that, "she who reigns over us has elected amid all the splendours of Empire to establish her life on the principle of domestic love."

The Prince's position had never been an easy one. Before their marriage the Queen had warned Prince Albert that "the English are very jealous of any foreigner interfering in the Government of this country." Very slowly did that jealousy abate. The Prince's patience and tact in trying circumstances were well-nigh irreproachable; yet not until he was gone did the nation at large

> . . . See him as he moved,
> How modest, kindly, all accomplished, wise,
> With what sublime repression of himself . . .

The Queen poured forth her grief in a series of passionate letters to King Leopold. He had made the match, and did his best to comfort the "utterly broken-hearted and crushed widow . . . whose life, as a happy one was ended." The Queen went into retirement from which she emerged only in the last two decades of her reign. She still worked assiduously at the business of State, but by her people was unseen. Nor was her sorrow without alleviation. In 1858 her eldest daughter, the Princess Royal, had made a marriage of affection with the Crown Prince of Prussia, and in 1863 her eldest son married the Princess Alexandra of Denmark.

Yet happy as both these marriages were, they still further complicated a problem already sufficiently embarrassing to the Queen and the British Government. In 1863 King Frederick VII of Denmark died. His nephew, Christian IX, father of the Princess of Wales, succeeded to the Danish throne without question: but his claim to Schleswig and Holstein was hotly disputed. Holstein was a German Duchy, Schleswig was largely German, but both Duchies had for centuries been held, in personal union, by Kings of Denmark.

Bismarck, who had lately become the Minister of Prussia, was determined to get them for Prussia. He induced Austria to pull the chestnuts out of the fire for him, and Russian neutrality he had assured by helping the Czar to quell the insurrection of his Poles in January 1863. England with the rest of the Powers had by Treaty (1852) guaranteed the "integrity" of the Danish kingdom, and the sympathies both of the Government and the people were decidedly in favour of the Danes. The Queen, on the contrary, championed the claims of Germany, if not of Prussia. Lord Palmerston shrewdly realized that the anxiety of Bismarck to grab the Duchies was inspired by "the dream of a German fleet, and the wish to get Kiel as a German sea-port," and at the close of the session of 1863 he announced that if any attempt were made to "overthrow the rights and violate the independence" of Denmark, "it would not be Denmark alone with which they would have to contend." But it was: Denmark was left to its fate. Palmerston might bluster; Russell's "fierce notes and pacific measures" (the phrase was Lord Salisbury's), while doing nothing to help Denmark, greatly lowered England's reputation on the Continent. Bismarck estimated Russell's homilies at their true value, and went on his way unheeding. Napoleon III, annoyed with England for refusing to join him in an attempt to succour Poland in 1863, would not help her to save the "Danish Duchies" in 1864. So Bismarck achieved his dual purpose: he got the Duchies for Prussia, and he fixed a quarrel on Austria, whom in 1866 he drove out of Germany and deprived of Venice.

The Queen felt her lonely position acutely. Pathetically she begged Lord Russell to give her more assistance "in her present desolation in forming her opinion on the various important questions affecting the foreign policy of this country." Her supreme anxiety, constantly reiterated, was to avert war between Germany and Denmark if possible, but in any case to prevent Great Britain from being involved in it. Whether, if unchecked by the Queen and the majority of the Cabinet, Palmerston and Russell would have actively intervened, is doubtful; but it is certain that their language greatly intensified the anxieties of the Queen.

Yet never for one moment was she deflected from her attitude of strict neutrality; and to her behaviour throughout the crisis Mr. Gladstone bore remarkable testimony. "Often," he wrote (January 4, 1864), "as I have been struck by the Queen's extraordinary integrity of mind . . . I never felt it more than on hearing and reading a letter of hers on Saturday (at the Cabinet) about the Danish question. Her determination, in this case as in others, not inwardly to 'sell the truth' . . . overbears all prepossessions and longings, strong as they are on the German side, and enables her spontaneously to hold the balance, it seems to me, tolerably even."

Again in 1866, the Queen made desperate efforts to avert

war between Prussia and the Germanic Confederation. In this case her domestic feelings were hopelessly divided. On the one side, the Crown Prince and Princess of Prussia; on the other, her cousin of Hanover; her brother-in-law of Saxe-Coburg and her son-in-law of Hesse. Her feelings were deeply harrowed and were not assuaged by the "crossness," the "petulant and irritated tone" of Lord Clarendon, who in 1865 had succeeded Lord Russell as Foreign Secretary.

For in that year a great event had happened. On October 18th Lord Palmerston had died and the Queen could "turn to no other but Lord Russell, an old and tried friend," to carry on the Government. He carried it on until June 1866, when, owing to his defeat on one of his many Reform Bills, he resigned office and retired from public life.

Lord Palmerston's death the Queen regretted as severing a link with "the past—the happy past," and she admitted that "in many ways he was a great loss." But to King Leopold she writes of him with characteristic frankness: "He had many valuable qualities, though many bad ones, and we had, God knows, terrible trouble with him about Foreign affairs. Still, as Prime Minister, he managed affairs at home well, and behaved to me well. But I *never* liked him, or could ever the least respect him, nor could I forget his conduct on certain occasions to my angel. He was very vindictive, and personal feelings influenced his political acts very much. Still, he is a loss."

Vindictive Palmerston was not; he was a bonny fighter; hot-tempered; impatient of opposition; and not always considerate to the Queen. If he ever felt a doubt that his own view was the correct one, he never betrayed it, but for a man so entirely self-confident he took the rubs of the political game with superb serenity. He had none of Russell's sensitiveness and self-consciousness. Though dismissed from the Foreign Office in 1851, he accepted with good-humour an inferior post in 1852, and in 1859 he was willing to serve under the much younger colleague who had supplanted him at the Foreign Office. Such conduct hardly argues "vindictiveness." Nor does vindictiveness make for popularity, either with intimates or with the public at large; and Palmerston enjoyed both in full measure. To the general public he was for two whole generations an outstanding figure in politics: the typical Englishman, overbearing, perhaps, towards foreigners, yet not on that account the less popular with his own countrymen. But his supreme endowment was his perennial youthfulness. Longevity is always a great asset in politics: combined with the elasticity and ebullience of youth it is irresistible. Palmerston obstinately refused to grow old. He was one of the happy few who are born young, and to the end he preserved the dew of his youth.

CHAPTER VII

LORD DERBY—THE NADIR OF CONSERVATISM

"He abolished slavery, he educated Ireland, he reformed Parliament." So Disraeli summarized the political career of the only chief under whom he ever served. The summary, though literally accurate, is characteristically grandiloquent, and conveys the impression that Lord Derby played in the politics of the Victorian era a much larger part than history can assign to him. Born in 1799, he lived out the allotted span and died in 1869. He was three times Prime Minister, though his tenure of the Premier's office covered an aggregate period of less than four years, and he never commanded a regular majority in the House of Commons. Educated at Eton and Christ Church, he left Oxford, like Lord Rosebery, without taking a degree, but, unlike Lord Rosebery, became Chancellor of the University (1852) and filled the office with great dignity until his death. The "Derby Scholarship," the highest classical distinction in the University, appropriately commemorates the fine scholarship of its Chancellor.

The eldest son of the thirteenth Earl of Derby, Edward Stanley[1] entered the House of Commons in the Whig interest in 1822 as member for Stockbridge; in 1826 he

[1] Edward Stanley, fourteenth Earl of Derby, b. 1799; ed. Eton and Christ Church; M.P. Stockbridge as Whig (1822–6); M.P. Preston (1826–30); Windsor (1831–2); South Lancs (1832–44); Under-Secretary for Colonies under Canning (1827); Chief Secretary for Ireland under Grey (1830–3); Colonial Secretary (1833–4), and under Peel (1841–5); Earl of Derby (1851); P.M. (1852, 1858–9, and 1866–8); d. 1869.

H. P. Briggs pinx. *H. Cousins sc.*

EDWARD STANLEY, 14TH EARL OF DERBY

was returned for the ancient borough of Preston—a family seat, and served his official apprenticeship as Under-Secretary for the Colonies under Canning. He refused office under Wellington, but accepted it as Chief Secretary for Ireland in the "Reform" Ministry of Lord Grey.

Though he led the Conservative Party for twenty years, Stanley was throughout life a typical Whig, and it was in the true spirit of Whiggism that he ruled Ireland from 1830 to 1833. He was honestly convinced that the best thing he could do for Ireland was to dose her with the remedies prescribed by the Whigs for England, and all would be well. Ireland, like England, should have an enlarged electorate and municipal self-government, a reformed Poor Law, and a national system of education. Stanley's Education Act of 1831 did indeed lay the foundations of elementary education in Ireland. But the actual structure contradicted the design. Stanley provided for a "mixed" system. On four days a week Protestant and Catholic children were side by side to learn their letters; on two days they were, separately, to imbibe religious instruction. This "rational" arrangement might suit a "rational" people: it did not suit the Irish, who were determined to have, and in fact quickly obtained, a purely denominational system. The shell of Stanley's scheme survived, but that only.

In 1832 Ireland got its share of the Reform Bill, and in 1838 a reformed Poor Law; in 1840 the Irish Municipal Bill at last became law, after six years of continuous controversy involving many bitter fights between the Upper and the Lower House. But the irony of the situation was that none of these Whig reforms, beneficent though they might be, made the slightest appeal to Irish sentiment. To the first reformed Parliament (1832) Ireland returned 38 Repealers, with Daniel O'Connell at their head; and of the 67 Unionists more than half advocated the abolition of tithes.

Consequently, Stanley found Ireland in the throes of a tithe-war. To the great mass of the people tithe was not merely an obnoxious financial impost, but a symbol of the political ascendancy of an alien and detested Church-establishment. "Let your hatred of tithe be as lasting as your love of justice." Such was the advice given by a Catholic prelate to the peasantry. It was promptly followed. No tithes were paid. Stanley tried to enforce the law; he strengthened it by his Coercion Act of 1833, but as an Irish peer confessed, "it is more safe to violate the law than to obey it." Eventually (in 1838) after a long contest a Tithe Commutation Act was passed.

Tithe was only one factor in a larger problem—the position of the English Church in Ireland. The Whig Ministry nibbled at the great question and in 1833 passed a Bill for the suppression of ten Irish bishoprics, the reduction of the larger clerical incomes and the abolition of many indefensible sinecures. This was the Act of "National Apostasy" which formed the text of Keble's famous sermon at Oxford (July 14, 1833), an event which is regarded as the birthday of the Tractarian Movement.

The Grey Cabinet was hopelessly divided on Irish questions. In 1834 it agreed to the appointment of a commission to inquire into the position of the Irish Church, whereupon Stanley, who in 1833 had left the Irish Office for the Colonial Office, resigned, and took with him Sir James Graham, the Earl of Ripon (Robinson) and the Duke of Richmond. The Government only survived their secession by a few months. The great "Reform" ship went to pieces on the Irish rocks.

Thus the "Whig" period of Stanley's strangely disjointed career came to an end; but not before he had made his tenure of the Colonial Office memorable by carrying a Bill for the "abolition of slavery throughout the British

Colonies." He refused office in the short-lived Ministry of Peel in 1834, but returned to the Colonial Office in that of 1841. Stanley had not yet (if he ever did) become a Conservative, and he was only a half-hearted Peelite. The crisis of his political fate came with Peel's decision to abolish the Corn Laws. For so sudden and sweeping a measure Stanley, though no full-blooded Protectionist, was not prepared, and Peel, deprived of his powerful support, resigned. Stanley offered to the Queen an elaborate explanation of his conduct; but it was coldly received and acknowledged with a curtness which betrayed the Queen's annoyance. The Queen gave "full credit to the disinterested motives which guided Lord Stanley's conduct," but she never quite forgave him for "deserting" her favourite Minister, and (virtually) depriving her of his services.

For the next six years Stanley led a rather ragged army of Protectionists from the House of Lords, to which in 1844 he had been called up by his father's Barony of Bickerstaffe. Feeling no confidence in his followers, he inspired little confidence among them. Lord George Bentinck he disliked and mistrusted; he was strongly prejudiced against Disraeli, and not until the summer of 1848 was there any approach to friendly personal relations between the two men who were destined at last to lead a reconstructed Conservative Party out of the wilderness in which for twenty years they had been wandering.

Had Stanley remained in the House of Commons he might have given to the history of the Conservative Party, perhaps to the history of his country, a wholly different turn. He had almost all the gifts required for parliamentary leadership. He was, it is true, if not haughty, inaccessible; but so was Peel; though not indolent, he was incapable of sustained industry; but he was at once a great orator and a brilliant debater—gifts rarely combined; he was an admirable man of business, and was quick to grasp the essential points of any question with which he had to deal. He was a strong Churchman of the Erastian type; an admirable landlord, and in his native Lancashire he was, like all the Stanleys, immensely and deservedly popular. During the cotton famine he not only subscribed generously to the fund for relief of distress, but as Chairman of the Committee gave ungrudgingly of his time and experience to its business. Yet he somehow failed, partly from the untoward political circumstances of his day, partly from the defects of his own qualities, to exercise such a decisive influence over the course of national affairs as might from his great talents have been anticipated.

The untowardness of circumstances is well illustrated by the events of 1850. Palmerston's conduct of foreign affairs was, as already indicated, causing great uneasiness among both friends and opponents, as well at the English as at Foreign Courts. On June 18 Stanley moved a vote of censure on the Government for their treatment of Greece, and, by the aid of one of the most brilliant speeches of his life, carried it in a full House by a majority of thirty-seven. In the House of Commons, however, the Government got a vote of confidence by a majority of fifty-four—a result due mainly to Palmerston's famous *Civis Romanus Sum* speech—a speech with which for five hours he held the House enthralled.

But the reprieve of the Ministry was of short duration, and on Russell's resignation in February 1851, the Queen summoned Stanley, who, as already described, found himself unable to form a Government. In that year he succeeded his father as Earl of Derby, and at the end of 1852, under circumstances already detailed, the new Earl was at last, and reluctantly, compelled to take office.

His field of choice for colleagues was lamentably limited.

Under the pressure of adversity Disraeli had been accepted as the leader of the Party in the House of Commons, but, with all his great talents, he had thus far failed to win the confidence of his followers. Six years of opposition had, however, failed to reveal in their ranks any possible competitor, and Disraeli became leader of the House and Chancellor of the Exchequer.

The Foreign Office was given to Lord Malmesbury, whose views were at any rate more acceptable to the Queen than his predecessor's. A general election in July gave the new Ministry the support of 299 members: but the Liberals numbered 315, and as the latter were generally supported by 40 Peelites, it was obvious that Lord Derby's tenure of office would be brief. The Prime Minister referred with satisfaction to his team of young horses: "not one had ever been in harness before and they went beautifully; not one among them kicked." The Queen, on the other hand, described it as "a very sorry Cabinet." It lasted, in fact, only long enough to enable Disraeli to introduce his Budget in December. Upon that Budget Gladstone made a terrific onslaught; the Government was defeated and, after holding office for just 300 days, resigned (December 18).

Lord Aberdeen's Coalition Ministry lasted until February 1855, and on its fall the Queen again sent for Lord Derby; but the latter failed to secure the co-operation of the Peelites, and without it declined to take office. In 1858, however, Lord Palmerston came to grief over the Conspiracy to Murder Bill, and Lord Derby could not longer refuse the responsibilities of office. His second Cabinet was a stronger one than the first. Lord Malmesbury, Disraeli, Mr. Walpole (Home Secretary), Mr. Henley (Board of Trade), and Lord John Manners (Office of Works) returned to their previous posts, and the inclusion of Lord Stanley (the Premier's eldest son) and General Jonathan Peel materially strengthened the

Government. General Peel, a brother of Sir Robert, proved himself an admirable Secretary of State for War. Lord Stanley, at first appointed to the Colonial Office, became, on the passing of the Government of India Bill, the first Secretary of State for India.

The Mutiny had brought the rule of the East India Company to an end. The transference of the great dependency to the direct government of the Crown proved, however, a ticklish business. Palmerston's Ministry had brought in a Bill to effect that object, but the new Government, prompted by Lord John Russell, preferred to proceed by way of resolution. The resolutions were, after close debate, embodied in a Bill which on August 2, 1858, received the Royal Assent. All the powers, territories and revenues of the Company were transferred to the Queen, who was to be represented in India by a Viceroy, while a Secretary of State, assisted by a Council, was to supersede the old Board of Control and its President, and to be responsible to Parliament for the conduct of Indian affairs.

On November 1, 1858, this momentous change was announced to the princes, chiefs and people of India by a Royal Proclamation, the terms of which were carefully revised by the Queen herself. With the first draft she was far from satisfied, and wrote to Lord Derby (August 15, 1858) as follows:

"The Queen has asked Lord Malmesbury to explain in detail to Lord Derby her objections to the draft of Proclamation for India. The Queen would be glad if Lord Derby would write it himself in his excellent language, bearing in mind that it is a female Sovereign who speaks to more than 100,000,000 of Eastern people on assuming the direct Government over them after a bloody civil war, giving them pledges which her future reign is to redeem, and explaining the principles of her Government. Such a document should breathe feelings of generosity, benevolence, and religious feeling, pointing out the privileges which the Indians will receive in being placed on an equality with the subjects of the British Crown, and the prosperity following in the train of civilization."

The Queen's wishes were precisely respected, and the Proclamation, in its final form, was worthy of an historic occasion.

To the princes of India the Queen announced that all engagements and treaties made with the Company would be scrupulously maintained. She renounced all ideas of conquest or "extension of our present territorial possessions," and in a memorable passage proceeded:

"While we will permit no aggression upon our dominions or our rights, to be attempted with impunity, we shall sanction no encroachment on those of others. We shall respect the rights, dignity, and honour of native princes as our own; and we desire that they, as well as our own subjects, should enjoy that prosperity and that social advancement which can only be secured by internal peace and good government."

But nowhere were the Queen's personal views revealed more clearly than in the passage with reference to religion:

"Firmly relying," said Her Majesty, "on the truth of Christianity, and acknowledging with gratitude the solace of religion, we disclaim alike the right and the desire to impose our convictions on any of our subjects. It is our Royal will and pleasure that no one shall in any wise suffer for his opinions, or be disquieted by reason of his religious faith or observance. We will show to all alike the equal and impartial protection of the law, and we do strictly charge and enjoin those who may be in authority under us that they abstain from all interference with the religious belief or worship of any of our subjects under pain of our highest displeasure. It is our further will that, so far as may be, our subjects, of whatever class or creed, be fully and freely admitted to any offices the duties of which they may be qualified by their education, abilities, and integrity duly to discharge." Finally, the Queen declared that the aim of her government should be the benefit of all her subjects resident in India. "In their prosperity will be our strength, in their contentment our security, and in their gratitude our best reward."

The proclamation produced the happiest effect in India, and the Queen's pleasure is reflected in a letter to Lord Canning, the Viceroy (December 2, 1858).

"It is," she writes, "a source of great satisfaction and pride to her to feel herself in direct communication with that enormous Empire which is so bright a jewel of her Crown, and which she would wish to see happy, contented, and peaceful. May the publication of her proclamation be the beginning of a new era, and may it draw a veil over the sad and bloody past."

Throughout the remainder of her reign the Queen's hopes were realized to the full.

With the foreign policy pursued by Lord Malmesbury the Queen was well pleased. Though strongly opposed to the "Italian" policy of Palmerston and Russell, and mistrustful of the schemes and ambitions of the French Emperor, the Foreign Secretary, like the Queen herself, was reduced to despair by the conduct of Austria. At his New Year's Day reception Napoleon had addressed M. Hübner, the Austrian Ambassador in Paris, in words which seemed to presage war.

That war the Queen and her Government did all in their power to avert. Their efforts were frustrated on the one hand by the pact between Napoleon and Cavour; on the other by the ineptitude of Austria, who seemed resolved to rush on her fate. "Austria is behaving with a folly which is perfectly inconceivable considering her position, surrounded by enemies on all the frontiers. But what can one expect of Buol! I care for neither Austria nor France; but Lord Derby and I are determined to use every effort to prevent war which would cost 100,000 lives and desolate the fairest parts of Europe." So Lord Malmesbury wrote on January 11 to the British Ambassador in Paris. Their efforts, as we have seen, failed.

Though at one with Lord Derby on foreign affairs, the Queen thought him insufficiently regardful of the prerogatives of the Crown. She had felt herself bound to pull him up sharply when in December 1852 he had presumed to offer advice about the selection of a successor. He had to be reminded somewhat sharply that, "constitutionally speaking, it did not rest with him to give advice and become responsible for it." Still more sharp was the reproof administered to him in July 1858:

"The Queen, in reading in the papers yesterday, on her way here from Camp, the debate in the House of Commons of the previous night, was shocked to find that in several important points her Government have surrendered the prerogatives of the Crown. She will only refer to the clauses concerning the Indian Civil Service and the right of peace and war.

"With respect to the first, the regulations under which servants of the Crown are to be admitted or examined have always been an undoubted right and duty of the Executive; by the clause introduced by Lord Stanley the system of

'Competitive Examination' has been confirmed by Act of Parliament. That system may be right or wrong; it has since its introduction been carried on under the Orders in Council; now the Crown and Government are to be deprived of any authority in the matter, and the whole examinations, selection, and appointments, etc., are to be vested in the Civil Commissioners under a Parliamentary title.

"As to the right of the Crown to declare war and make peace, it requires not a word of remark; yet Lord Stanley agrees to Mr. Gladstone's proposal to make over this prerogative with regard to Indian questions to Parliament under the auspices of the Queen's Government; she is thus placed in a position of less authority than the President of the American Republic."

Nor was the Queen inclined to renounce all responsibility for the terms in which she was made to address the new Parliament in the "Queen's speech," on June 7, 1859. To more than one paragraph in the draft speech the Queen took serious objection and insisted on their modification. Her alterations were undeniably improvements, but the pertinent point is that she refused to have put into her mouth words which she did not approve.

On another point, not less important, there was a decided difference of opinion between the Queen and her Prime Minister.

In May 1858, when the defeat of the Government appeared to be imminent, Lord Derby asked the Queen's permission to announce that in the event of an adverse majority he had the Queen's sanction to a dissolution of Parliament. The Queen refused to give that, or any other pledge, in advance. Most properly, she held that such an announcement would be an unconstitutional threat to Parliament.

So important did the question seem to the Queen that

she privately consulted Lord Aberdeen about it. Aberdeen held that the Government had a perfect right to threaten a dissolution in the event of their defeat but not to "join the Queen's name with it." He further held that if the Minister advised the Queen to dissolve, "she would as a matter of course do so." He did not deny that it lay within "the power and prerogative of the Sovereign to refuse a Dissolution"; it was, as he truly said, "one of the very few acts which the Queen of England could do without responsible advice at the moment"; but he pointed out that the incoming Minister, whoever he might be, would have to assume responsibility retrospectively for the Queen's refusal, and strongly advised the Queen, under the circumstances, not to adopt an "unusual" and, as he believed, "unprecedented" course.

The point of prerogative has been frequently raised between Colonial Governors and their responsible advisers, and might well have been raised, if it has not, on at least two recent occasions in England. Mr. Asquith in December 1923 expressed himself unequivocally in favour of the Royal Prerogative, and to deny it would seem to deprive the Sovereign of one of the few reserve powers which may still need to be exercised in the interests, not of any particular Party, but of the Commonwealth.

For the rest, the Queen's relations with Lord Derby were, if less easy than with Melbourne or Peel, Aberdeen or Disraeli, sufficiently friendly, and when, in June 1859, he resigned, she gave him the Garter, an unusual honour when there was no vacancy in the Order.

It was seven years before Lord Derby returned to office, but when, on the defeat of the Russell Ministry in June 1866, he formed his third Administration, it was incomparably stronger in personnel than any Conservative Ministry since the Reform Bill. Lord Carnarvon came in as Colonial and

Viscount Cranborne (afterwards the third Marquis of Salisbury) as Indian Secretary. The Queen would have preferred Lord Carnarvon to Lord Stanley for the Foreign Office; even his father did not pretend that the latter was specially well suited to it, and tried to induce Lord Clarendon to retain his post, but despite the efforts both of the Queen and the new Prime Minister, Clarendon refused to quit his party ("because allegiance to party is the only strong political feeling I have"). Him failing, Lord Derby thought his son better fitted for the office than anyone else. The Adullamites—the Liberal group opposed to Reform—refused to join the Ministry, so did Lord Shaftesbury, whose adhesion was greatly desired as "the best answer to the allegation that the Conservative Party was indifferent to the case of the 'working man'." But the Cabinet, though formed exclusively of Conservatives, was particularly strong in recruits, such as Lord Cranborne, Sir Stafford Northcote and Gathorne Hardy, all of whom were destined to play important parts in politics during the ensuing thirty years.

The new Ministry lasted, though in a minority, and in days rendered decidedly "unquiet," by Hyde Park demonstrations and Fenian outrages, for two years and a half. It is more to the point that during its brief existence it placed on the statute-book two measures of first-rate importance: the *British North America Act* and the second great instalment of Parliamentary Reform.

The former Act marked an important stage in the evolution of Colonial Self-government. Canada had attained to "Responsible Government" soon after the *Union Act* of 1840; but Canada (then consisting of Quebec and Ontario) was not the only British possession in North America. To Newfoundland, Prince Edward Isle, Nova Scotia, and New Brunswick on the Atlantic coast, there had lately been added British Columbia, on the Pacific. That these colonies, each relatively small, could continue to exist in isolation, side by side with the Republic of the United States, seemed to the wiser Canadian statesmen improbable. A movement in favour of a Confederation under the British Crown made rapid headway between 1864 and 1867, and in December 1866 delegates representing Quebec, Ontario, Nova Scotia and New Brunswick met in conference in London, under Lord Carnarvon's presidency. Terms were agreed, and embodied in the Bill which in 1867 became law as the *British North America Act*. The Queen received, with full State ceremonial, the delegates from the Colonies, and agreed that the new Confederation should be officially designated the *Dominion of Canada*. It was also at her suggestion that the territory on the Pacific, which joined the Confederation in 1871, should be christened British Columbia.[1]

The change of political emphasis in the last sixty years is strikingly illustrated by the relative degree of attention bestowed by contemporaries on Canadian Federation and the Household Suffrage Bill respectively. The latter not merely absorbed the attention of Parliament from February to August; it involved the secession of three leading members of the Cabinet—Lord Cranborne, Lord Carnarvon and General Peel. General Grey, who, on the Prince Consort's death, became Private Secretary to the Queen, reported to her (? February 12) that "Mr. Disraeli made a great mess of it to-night." On the 25th Lord Derby reported that "the Government has been this day on the point of an ignominious disruption," though the ignominy, if not the disruption, was in his opinion averted. Yet the Queen

[1] For details about the Federal Constitution of Canada, see Marriott, *Mechanism of the Modern State*, Vol. I, c. ix; and *Second Chambers* (revised edition, 1927), c. vii.

found him on the 27th "in terribly low spirits." Her own supreme anxiety was that the Reform question might be settled "for many years to come, with the assent of all parties," and that an agreed measure might be passed without involving a ministerial crisis. There was indeed nothing, except possibly war, which the Queen dreaded and disliked so much as a change of Ministers—even for the better.

Household suffrage, without any of the checks, balances, and safeguards originally proposed, became the law of the land, and 1,000,000 new voters—more than twice as many as in 1832—received the franchise. Lord Derby (privately) expressed a hope that "he had dished the Whigs." Publicly he commended the Bill—rather oddly for a Conservative —as a "leap in the dark." Carlyle, with characteristic mistrust of Parliamentary Democracy, described Disraeli's feat as "shooting Niagara."

The passing of the Bill brought Lord Derby's career to a close. He retired from the Premiership, on the ground of failing health, in February 1868, and died in 1869. He was a man of brilliant parts; admirable in all relations of life; pre-eminently a great Englishman, but not as a statesman in the front rank. Still, the Queen parted from him with "extreme reluctance," assured him that she had found in his service as First Minister "comfort and support," and wished him to remain in the Cabinet even without portfolio, since his name was a "tower of strength" to his party. But Lord Derby's course was run.

As to the choice of a successor there could be no question. Without one day's delay, and with a minimum of personal disturbance, Disraeli took over the reins. The new Minister thought it necessary to strengthen his Government in the Lords; so Sir Hugh Cairns, a brilliant Ulster lawyer, received a peerage and replaced Lord Chelmsford on the

Woolsack. Mr. Ward Hunt, a country gentleman who had been a successful Secretary to the Treasury, became, in Disraeli's place, Chancellor of the Exchequer.

Before the new Government had been a month in office, Mr. Gladstone brought forward his resolutions for the Disestablishment of the Irish Church. An amendment moved from the Treasury Bench was defeated by a majority of 61, and on April 30 Gladstone carried by a similar majority the first of his resolutions. Disraeli at once tendered his resignation, but the Queen refused to accept it, and on May 4 the Minister announced that the Queen had alternatively sanctioned a dissolution of Parliament as soon as the business of the Session could be wound up.

The Opposition received this announcement with deep chagrin, and denounced the tactics which inspired it as unconstitutional—the characteristic device of a political mountebank. Mr. Gladstone resented any delay in the accomplishment of the great task to which he had now put his hands, and carried through the House of Commons a Bill suspending until August 1, 1869, the exercise of the public ecclesiastical patronage in Ireland. The Lords, however, after a brilliant speech against the Bill from Lord Derby, decisively rejected it, and insisted that so great an issue should be referred to the new Electorate.

The constituencies gave Gladstone an immense majority, and Disraeli promptly resigned (December 4), without awaiting the meeting of Parliament. The Queen regarded this unusual course as "less painful to herself and more dignified for the Ministers themselves."

Thereupon, Mr. Gladstone became for the first time Prime Minister and remained in office until 1874.

CHAPTER VIII

BENJAMIN DISRAELI, EARL OF BEACONSFIELD —THE CONSERVATIVE REVIVAL

"POWER! It has come to me too late."[1] In a sense Disraeli was right. Not until 1868 was he the acknowledged leader of his own Party; not until 1874 did the voice of the country call him to power. By that time he was close on seventy. Prematurely aged; broken in body and in spirits; deprived by death of the devoted wife who for thirty years had given him not merely a home, but the female adulation essential to his happiness; he had at long last reached the summit of ambition, only to find it enveloped in cloud.

To all his contemporaries Disraeli was an enigma; to most of them he was an extravagance; to not a few he was an actual affront. An enigma he will to all time remain; but we are at least in a better position to unravel it than were his contemporaries. We can see his career in perspective, and judge it as a whole. Men viewing it from different angles still arrive at conclusions widely divergent; yet on one point there is unanimity: it is agreed that in the history of English politics Disraeli occupies a place that is unique.

"Un-English" was the epithet most frequently applied by hostile critics, alike to his personality and his policy. Among the ingredients of his character there were indeed many which are rarely bestowed on Englishmen—notably

[1] Benjamin Disraeli, Earl of Beaconsfield, b. 1804; M.P. Maidstone (1837); Shrewsbury (1841–7); Bucks (1847–76); Chancellor of Exchequer (1852), and Leader of H. of C. (1858–9 and 1866–8); P.M. (1868 and 1874–80). Earl of Beaconsfield (1876); K.G. (1878); d. 1881.

that of imagination. But if he was "un-English," no Englishman ever loved England better, admired her more fervently, or served her, according to his lights, with more unswerving devotion. "Zeal for the greatness of England" was, indeed, as Lord Salisbury declared, "the passion of his life." "I am neither Whig nor Tory; my politics are described by one word, and that word is England." So Disraeli himself wrote in the *Gallomania* some years before he set foot in the House of Commons. It was no mere flight of rhetoric; it was the recital of a creed to which throughout his career he remained constant. Yet Disraeli was in one sense a strong party man; with Burke he held that without party organization, parliamentary government were impossible. Nevertheless, Party occupied, in his scheme of things, a subordinate place. Parties may come and go; they may vacate this position and occupy that; they may interchange watchwords, and adopt to-day the policy which yesterday they decried; they may abandon leaders and betray followers; they may confuse tactics with principles, and exalt shibboleths into eternal truths; but, through all their mutations, and despite recriminations, England remains. Such was the creed of the young Hebrew adventurer; such was the faith which sustained him in all the changes and chances of a career singularly chequered; the faith by which he lived, in which he died.

If zeal for the greatness of England was the passion of Disraeli's life, he shared it with his Sovereign. That was the real bond of union between them. Some ridicule has been cast upon the relations of the Queen and her Minister. Not unnaturally, in view of Disraeli's epistolary style. That was, indeed, "un-English"; but the basis of their mutual attraction and admiration was common devotion to the interests, as they saw them, of the country they served.

It was not, however, until he became Prime Minister that the Queen began to appreciate Disraeli, or to discern the great qualities which lay hidden under his eccentricities. The first mention of him in the Queen's *Letters* was in terms far from complimentary. She was "a little shocked at Sir Charles Wood . . . designating the *future Government* and selecting Lord George Bentinck, Mr. Disraeli (!) and Mr. Herries as the persons destined to hold *high office* in the next Government" (December 19, 1847). Writing to Lord Stanley in 1851, she sorrowfully admitted that "if there was a Protectionist Government Mr. Disraeli must be the Leader of the House of Commons"; and then added with emphasis: "I do not approve of Mr. Disraeli. I do not approve of his conduct to Sir Robert Peel." That was the real rock of offence: his attack upon the Minister she trusted. Lord Stanley tried to mitigate the Queen's displeasure by pointing out that "men who have to make their position will say and do things which are not necessary to be said or done by those for whom positions are provided." The Queen agreed; she promised not to aggravate Lord Stanley's difficulties in Cabinet-making by vetoing Disraeli's appointment, but she insisted that if she admitted him to office Lord Stanley must make himself "responsible for his conduct." Stanley undertook the responsibility, and so in 1852 the "damned bumptious Jew boy" became, without any official apprenticeship, Chancellor of the Exchequer and leader of the House of Commons.

Disraeli was now forty-seven. Born on December 21, 1804, he was only just of age when he leapt into notoriety as the author of a brilliantly audacious novel—*Vivian Grey*. By descent an Italian Jew, he had been baptized as a member of the Church of England at the age of twelve, and to the ordinances of that Church he consistently conformed throughout life. But Disraeli's religion, like everything else about him, was *sui generis*: he was his own standard and his own exemplar. The principle of race, so he constantly insisted, is "the key of history"; to him it was also the basis of religion. "Christianity," he said, "is completed Judaism or it is nothing." His Christianity derived from the fact that Christ was a Jew. Perhaps the noblest passage that Disraeli ever penned is the peroration to the chapter on the Jewish Question in the *Life of Lord George Bentinck*. Evidently written with his heart's blood, it makes a passionate appeal to the Jews to accept Christianity as the natural evolution of Hebraism. ". . . in this enlightened age, as his mind expands and he takes a comprehensive view of this period of progress, the pupil of Moses may ask himself whether all the princes of the house of David have done so much for the Jews as the Prince who was crucified on Calvary? . . . Has He not made their history the most famous in the world? . . . Has not He avenged the victory of Titus and conquered the Cæsars? What successes did they anticipate from their Messiah? The wildest dreams of their rabbis have been far exceeded" (Chapter XXIV).

As regards that "pure reformed and apostolic branch of the Catholic Church established in these realms," Disraeli's position was clear. "There were few great things left in England," so he wrote in his Preface to *Lothair* (1870), "and the Church was one." The Church ministered to the spiritual side of man as against the material, and Disraeli was ever "on the side of the angels" against the apes. But the Church was also a bulwark of ordered Society, and as such it must be maintained, on the one hand against the external assaults of Dissent; on the other against the disintegrating forces of Ritualism and Latitudinarianism. This does not mean that Disraeli was theologically an evangelical, though the *Public Worship*

Regulation Act (1874) and most of his ecclesiastical appointments might have seemed to indicate it. He was, in fine, a Christian Jew and an Erastian: as a Conservative he regarded religion and the Established Church as among the most potent of the forces that sustained the State.

The Queen's views did not, in this matter, differ widely from Disraeli's. To ritualism she was even more strongly opposed than he was. She would not allow Lord Salisbury to make Canon Liddon Bishop of Oxford lest he should "ruin and taint all the young men as Pusey and others did before him" (July 6, 1888). But on the other hand she refused to have Dr. Ellicott, a pronounced Evangelical, as Archbishop of Canterbury, and frequently warned her Ministers that in ecclesiastical appointments they must think of the Church as a *national* institution and not allow party prepossessions, whether political or theological, to prevail.

But this is to anticipate. Disraeli had a long furrow to plough before he was in a position to make Bishops. This narrative is not, however, concerned with the earlier part of Disraeli's romantic and chequered career: with his literary adventures; his repeated but unsuccessful attempts to enter the House of Commons; his successful assault upon the citadel of "Society"; with his election, as Member for Maidstone, to the first Parliament of the new reign (1837); his marriage, two years later, to a wealthy widow, Mrs. Wyndham Lewis; his maiden speech in Parliament, less of a "failure" than is commonly supposed; his patient efforts to retrieve it; the formation of the "Young England Party"; his revolt against Peel and his bitter attack on the man whose whole life had been "one huge appropriation clause"; on the "Turkish Admiral who steered his fleet into the enemy's port." Are not all these things written in the Book of the Chronicles of Monypenny and Buckle?

The revolt against Sir Robert Peel marked the real beginning of Disraeli's political career. In *Tancred*, published about the same time (1847), he summarized his political philosophy and prefigured his political programme. That novel expands and illustrates the argument of his more formal treatise, *A Vindication of the English Constitution*. The primary object of both works was to discredit the "Whig oligarchy" established in power by the Revolution of 1688, and to indicate the claim of the Tories to be a truly national party.

Disraeli's first business, then, was to "educate" his party, as that of Bolingbroke had been a century earlier. Like Bolingbroke, he wanted to "dish the Whigs" and on the ruins of the territorial oligarchy to re-establish a popular monarchy—a *Patriot King*. Disraeli's novels, like the philosophical treatises of Bolingbroke, were political pamphlets under a thin disguise; and, as such, they were extraordinarily effective. The new Toryism, as expounded in *Coningsby*, *Sybil* and *Tancred*, was based on the triple foundation of "Altar, Throne, and Cottage." That was, in essence, the programme with which he first appealed to the reformed electorate as Prime Minister in 1868. On it was based the policy of the Ministry he formed in 1874.

Once more we anticipate: but Disraeli's political career is so much a political whole that it tempts to the neglect of chronology, and perhaps justifies it. To return. The process of education was a prolonged one. It was by no means completed when in 1851, on the resignation of Lord John Russell, the Queen first sent for Lord Stanley. Stanley was convinced that he could not form a Government except with the help of the Peelites. Gladstone, however, would not join any Ministry which was not wholly free from the taint of Protection; there were other difficulties of personnel, and Stanley rather petulantly abandoned the attempt to form a Government.

It was resumed a year later when, as we have seen, Disraeli became Chancellor of the Exchequer. On March 15, 1852, he wrote his first letter to the Queen as leader of the House. The style of his letters somewhat startled the Sovereign, who wrote to King Leopold: "Mr. Disraeli (alias Dizzy) writes very curious reports to me of the House of Commons proceedings—much in the style of his books." But she soon came to appreciate the contrast they presented to the stereotyped form hitherto adopted. They provided, however, only a brief interlude. The new Ministry was out before the end of the year, and on the fall of the Coalition (1855) Derby missed an excellent chance of coming in again. Disraeli was deeply chagrined. One of his earlier biographers described the incident as "the greatest disappointment of his life." He regarded Derby's refusal to take office without the help of either Palmerston or Gladstone, not unnaturally, as a slur upon himself, but he was much more concerned at the blow thus inflicted on the prospects of a party which he had so patiently "educated."

In 1858 Lord Derby formed his second administration. Again Disraeli became Chancellor of the Exchequer and leader of the House, but not without an attempt to bring back Mr. Gladstone to his original allegiance. It was then that Disraeli wrote one of the most generous and manly letters ever addressed by any statesman to a rival and an opponent.[1] Gladstone frigidly declined Disraeli's advances.

Disraeli's second tenure of office, though longer than the first (February 1858 to June 1859), did little to increase his personal reputation. He had the satisfaction of seeing a Bill become law enabling Jews to sit in Parliament; but

[1] See Buckle: *Life*, IV, 157–8.

his own ill-devised and ill-timed Bill for parliamentary reform compelled an appeal to the country, and the Ministry did not long survive it. The greater by contrast was the success with which Disraeli piloted the Bill of 1867 through the House of Commons. The Conservatives, as already mentioned, had in the summer of 1866 for the third time taken office in a minority. Nor was the extra-parliamentary situation propitious. There was much distress among the lower-paid wage-earners; the London mob assumed a menacing attitude; the cattle-plague was making terrible ravages in all parts of Great Britain; a great firm of bill-discounters, Messrs. Overend, Gurney & Co., stopped payment with liabilities of £19,000,000 (May 1866); their failure was followed by a serious financial crisis and an epidemic of bankruptcies; the Fenian conspiracy, wide-spread in Ireland, extended its activities to England; an aborted attack on Chester Castle was followed by an affray in Manchester and a bomb outrage in Clerkenwell. These symptoms seemed to Mr. Gladstone to point to the presence of organic disease. To cure it he proposed to disestablish and disendow the Irish Church. That proposal, as we saw, brought the first Disraeli Ministry to an end.

Disraeli's Ministry it had become on Lord Derby's resignation in February 1868. By this time the Queen was rapidly overcoming her dislike of "Disraeli." As late as November 1866 he was still "strange" though "amiable and clever." Six months later she had decided that he was "evidently the directing mind of the Ministry," and on Lord Derby's resignation she had no hesitation in making him the First Minister of the Crown. General Grey, the Queen's Private Secretary, reported most favourably on his conduct at this important juncture in his career. He "found Mr. Disraeli very cordial and *most* practical in all he said; going straight to the point, and showing a most sincere desire to do nothing that could look presumptuous on his part or unhandsome towards Lord Derby."

Disraeli's first letter to the Queen as Prime Minister was a masterpiece of tact. His delight he did not attempt to conceal; but in return for Her Majesty's "condescension" he could "only offer devotion." He hoped to spare Her Majesty as much trouble as possible in matters of unimportant detail, but he trusted that "in the great affairs of state" Her Majesty would "deign not to withhold from him the benefit" of her guidance. He then proceeded: "Your Majesty's life has been passed in constant communion with great men, and the knowledge and management of important transactions. Even if your Majesty were not gifted with those great abilities, which all now acknowledge, this rare and choice experience must give your Majesty an advantage in judgment which few living persons and probably no living prince can rival." Every word in these sentences went straight to the heart of the Queen. How different from the language of the Russells and Palmerstons and even the Derbys! Moreover, flattering as the words were, they were true. No wonder that Disraeli's advance in the Queen's regard was rapid. Yet her critical faculties were not dulled by adulation. When the Prime Minister wrote to her on the subject of royal visits to Ireland he was promptly and sternly rebuked. He observed very truly that there is "a great yearning in Ireland for the occasional presence and inspiration of Royalty"; he pointed out that during the last two centuries the Sovereign had only passed twenty-one days in Ireland, and suggested that perhaps the Prince of Wales might "hunt in the counties of Kildare and Meath and occupy a suitable residence."

The Queen would not hear of it. "In the Prince of

Wales's case," she wrote, "*any encouragement* of his constant love of running about and not keeping at home or near the Queen is *most earnestly and seriously* to be deprecated." Still, she allowed him to pay a short visit to Ireland though "*much regretting* that it should coincide with the Punchestown Races, as it naturally strengthens the belief" (so she wrote to the Prince himself), "already far too prevalent, that your chief object is amusement."

Mr. Gladstone's Irish Church resolutions caused the Queen, as the next chapter will show, the "deepest concern," but she urged her Tory Ministers "carefully to avoid saying anything, however great the provocation may be to act otherwise, that can tend to encourage a spirit of retaliation among the Protestants," to show "moderation and forbearance and studiously avoid taking a course which, though it might give them a party advantage for the moment, would surely be injurious to the permanent interests of the nation." More admirable and timely advice could not have been given.

Of the wise restraint imposed by the Queen upon the Minister's ecclesiastical appointments, mention has already been made. It was entirely due to her that at this critical juncture (1868) Dr. Tait, and not Dr. Ellicott, was appointed to the Archbishopric of Canterbury. Ultimately the Queen was satisfied that Disraeli, who was now "extremely agreeable and original," would "make good Church appointments as he sees the force of my arguments in favour of moderate and distinguished men" (September 20, 1868).

In a totally different department the Queen's good judgment saved Disraeli from a serious blunder.

Disraeli asked for a large grant of honours on the eve of the General Election. The Queen most wisely refused. She did not seek to conceal from her Minister her dislike of his rival's policy, but she called "his serious attention" to the supreme unwisdom of her consenting to a grant of "Honours" avowedly for the purpose of influencing elections which are to determine the fate of a Ministry." That would have "an appearance of partisanship," a thing of which she had always "endeavoured to steer clear."

The Election was a triumph for Mr. Gladstone, and Disraeli resigned without waiting for the meeting of Parliament, thus creating a precedent which has been generally followed. "Nothing," wrote General Grey to the Queen, "could have been more proper or manly than his way of taking what he admits to be a total defeat." One parting favour he asked of the Queen, a peerage in her own right for Mrs. Disraeli, who, being now seventy-six, could hardly hope to see her husband again in office. The Queen, though somewhat embarrassed, it would seem, by the unusual request, complied with it in the most cordial terms. Marital devotion she was always quick to appreciate; and no one could doubt that that of the Disraelis was mutual and genuine. Moreover, the Queen parted from Disraeli, brief as had been his term of office, with real regret, and expressed to him with evident sincerity "her deep sense of [his] great kindness and consideration towards her, not only in what concerned her personally, but in listening to her wishes—which were, however (she characteristically added), always prompted by the sole desire to promote the good of her country."

Despite his crushing defeat at the Polls, Disraeli had now a hold on the Tory Party such as no statesman had enjoyed since the death of Pitt. Of his superb leadership of the Opposition this is not, however, the place to speak. When in March 1873 Gladstone was defeated on his Irish University Bill, Disraeli refused to take office in the existing House of Commons. On every ground his refusal was justified. On the eve of the meeting of Parliament in

1874, Mr. Gladstone announced a Dissolution, and in the new House of Commons the Tories had a clear majority of over 50, reckoning all the Home Rulers, 58 strong, as opponents.

Mr. Gladstone, deferring to the opinions of his colleagues, at once resigned, and for the second time Disraeli kissed hands as Prime Minister.

Power had come to him at long last. For the first time since 1841 the Tories had a majority in the House of Commons. By general acknowledgment that majority was the product of one man's patience and sagacity. To what use would he put it?

Disraeli's Cabinet was limited to twelve members, six in either House, and was an exceptionally strong one. Lord Cairns returned to the Woolsack; the "deserters" of 1867 were readmitted to the bosom of the Party, as Secretaries of State: Lord Salisbury for India and Lord Carnarvon for the Colonies. Lord Derby went to the Foreign Office; Mr. Gathorne Hardy to the War Office, and Mr. Ward Hunt to the Admiralty. The last died in 1877 and was succeeded by "a Mr. Smith of Westminster, a rich and most respectable, clever man who always maintained that the working classes were *not* republican." The Queen's description of the man who was some day (1887–91) to lead the House of Commons raises a doubt whether the great lady who had never seen a railway ticket was aware that her newspapers were bought from Mr. W. H. Smith!

Sir Stafford Northcote, trained in the best traditions of Gladstonian finance, became Chancellor of the Exchequer; but the dark horse of the Cabinet was a shrewd, level-headed Lancashire man, Mr. R. A. Cross, who scored a brilliant success as Home Secretary, and became, and until her death remained, a close personal friend of the

Queen. In 1868 Cross had inflicted a sensational defeat on Gladstone in south-west Lancashire, and, though he had never held office, he had a large experience both of the Bar and of banking, and had sat in the House of Commons intermittently since 1857. He was not the type of man who makes history, but, more than any other member except its chief, he gave the new Ministry its distinctive quality. *Sanitas, Sanitatum, omnia Sanitas,* had been the text of some of Disraeli's most effective election speeches. Opponents derided it as a policy of sewage, but Cross translated the phrase into fact, and by passing into law such Acts as the Factory Act (1878), the Public Health Act, Artisans Dwellings Act, Employers and Workmen Act (1875), Trades Union Act (1876), and Friendly Societies Act (1875), gave to the Conservative Party a hold on the confidence of the better-class artisan, that has never been wholly lost.

On the part of the Prime Minister social reform was not merely improvised as an electioneering cry. It represented the fulfilment of an ambition which had consistently inspired him from his first entrance into politics. It was foreshadowed in his earlier novels; it was fundamental to that new ideal of Toryism which he sought to impress upon his Party, and to which he had laboured to convert the country. But memorable as this great Ministry is for its record in social legislation, it is by its conduct of foreign and colonial affairs that it is even better remembered.

"Yes," said Bismarck, "this is a new age; a new world." It was true. Historians are beginning to realize that the later decades of the nineteenth century marked one of the great watersheds of modern history. With the 'seventies we passed into the era of world-politics (*Welt-Politik*). Of English statesmen Disraeli was the first to realize this profoundly significant development, and to base his policy upon it. In speech after speech he dilated upon this truth. "You have," he said, "a new world, new influences at work, new and unknown objects and dangers with which to cope. . . . The relations of England to Europe are not the same as they were in the days of Lord Chatham or Frederick the Great. The Queen of England has become the Sovereign of the most powerful of Oriental states. On the other side of the globe there are now establishments belonging to her teeming with wealth and population. . . . These are vast and novel elements in the distribution of power. . . . What our duty is, at this critical juncture, is to maintain the Empire of England."

It was Egypt that first claimed his attention. Hitherto England had been curiously indifferent to Egypt. The Cape of Good Hope, not the Isthmus of Suez, had been regarded as the vital link in the chain of our communications with India and the East. Since the advent of the Turks the old trade-routes had been blocked, and the Mediterranean, which for centuries had been the highway of commerce, had sunk into the position of a backwater. Napoleon had from the outset of his career regarded Egypt as the nerve-centre of the Empire on whose destruction he was bent. The Czar Nicholas had twice tried to persuade Great Britain to take Egypt and give Russia a free hand in the Balkans. Ferdinand de Lesseps endeavoured to interest English statesmen and financiers in his scheme for cutting the isthmus by a canal. All to no purpose. England obstinately averted her gaze from Egypt.

In 1869, however, the Suez Canal was opened. England had not contributed a shilling to its construction; but from the first it was her tonnage which provided the bulk of its revenue. In November 1875 Disraeli learnt that the 176,602 shares held by the Khedive Ismail were for sale. He decided to buy them. His Cabinet hesitated; but the Queen cordially approved. With the help of the Rothschilds the money (some £4,000,000) was found, and with lightning rapidity the transaction was concluded. On November 24—less than ten days after the matter was first mooted—Disraeli wrote jubilantly to the Queen: "It is just settled: you have it, Madam. The French Government has been outgeneralled. They tried too much, offering loans . . . with conditions that would have virtually given them the Government of Egypt." The Queen shared Disraeli's jubilation. The purchase, she wrote, "gives us complete security for India . . . an immense thing. . . . It is *entirely* the doing of Mr. Disraeli, who has *very large ideas*, and *very lofty views* of the position this country should hold. His mind is so much greater, larger, and his apprehension of things, great or small, so much quicker than that of Mr. Gladstone." King Leopold described Disraeli's *coup* as "the greatest event in modern politics." The Crown Princess of Prussia wrote warm congratulations to her mother and quoted a letter from her schoolboy son Willy: "I know you will be so delighted that England has bought the Suez Canal. How jolly." Twenty years later the views of the schoolboy were appreciably modified. When the Bill for the transaction was presented to Parliament in 1876 it was bitterly attacked by Gladstone and Robert Lowe: but on every ground, financial, political and strategic, Disraeli's brilliant *coup* has been abundantly justified.

It was not of the financial bargain that Disraeli thought. The purchase of the shares was only one item in a large policy. In 1875–6 the Queen reluctantly agreed ("with much anxiety and apprehension") to allow the Prince of Wales to visit India. The visit took place in the winter of 1875–6, and was an unqualified success. On February 8, 1876, the Queen (for the second time only since her widowhood) opened Parliament in person, and in her speech announced the intention of the Government to propose a "formal addition to the style and titles of the Sovereign."

The proposal to confer upon the Queen the title "Empress of India" aroused furious opposition both in Parliament and the country. The writer has in his possession a contemporary pamphlet "by the author of Ginx's Baby" entitled: *The Blot on the Queen's Head; or How Little Ben, The Head Waiter, Changed the Sign of The "Queen's Inn" to "Empress Hotel Limited," and The Consequences Thereof.* Extravagant in terms, the pamphlet accurately represents contemporary opinion. The Queen regarded the agitation as "disgraceful . . . *most disrespectful* and indecorous" and "mainly inspired by a desire to injure her Prime Minister." But the Queen and her Minister were equally determined not to yield "*to mere clamour* and intimidation" (the Queen's own words); and the Bill was carried, despite fierce opposition, by large majorities. The clamour was senseless and mainly manufactured; the assumption of the title was welcomed by the Indian princes, and the policy has entirely justified itself. "You can only act upon the opinion of Eastern nations through their imagination." So Disraeli had said at the time of the Mutiny. In moving the second reading of the Royal Titles Bill he said: "It is desired in India; it is anxiously expected. The princes and natives of India . . . know exactly what it means, and they know that what it means is what they wish." On January 1, 1877, at a great Durbar at Delhi, in the presence of over seventy ruling princes and chiefs, of some three hundred native noblemen and gentlemen, of the heads of all the Indian Government, of envoys from neighbouring lands, and a vast concourse of the Indian peoples, the Viceroy proclaimed Queen Victoria Kaisar-i-Hind, and she was saluted by the Maharajah Scindia, on behalf of the Indian princes, as Shah-in-Shah Padishah, Monarch of Monarchs.

of who?
of all?

princes - yes
natives - no?

Proclamation-day was celebrated by a dinner-party at Windsor, to which the Prime Minister and Lord George Hamilton, as acting Secretary of State for India, were bidden. "The Faery," wrote the former to Lady Bradford, "is much excited about the doings at Delhi. They have produced great effect in India, and indeed throughout the world, and triumphantly vindicate the policy of the measure which was so virulently, but so fruitlessly, opposed." Lord George Hamilton records that the Queen, usually so simple in dress, appeared at dinner that night "a mass of Oriental jewellery, mostly consisting of very large uncut stones and pearls, gifts from the ruling princes of India in 1858. The Prime Minister, with appropriate neglect of etiquette, proposed the health of the Empress of India "with a little speech as flowery as the oration of a Maharajah"; to which the Queen responded with a "pretty smiling bow and half a curtsey." A unique incident on a unique occasion.

Meanwhile, the Prime Minister had gone to the House of Lords as Earl of Beaconsfield. The promotion was well deserved, and was, indeed, rendered necessary by the Premier's failing health. Nevertheless, the coincidence between the gift of a Crown and the grant of a Coronet was perhaps unfortunate. "One good turn deserves another" was the subject of a *Punch* cartoon, which, then as always, precisely reflected the general sense.

Apart from the Royal Titles Bill, the Ministerial ship had been encountering heavy weather. The Balkan volcano was again giving signs of an impending eruption. The Crimean War had given the Turk a respite, a chance to put his house in order. True to tradition, he neglected it, and in 1875 the whole Eastern question was reopened by an insurrection among the peoples of Bosnia and Herzegovina, supported by volunteers from Serbia and Montenegro. It spread to Bulgaria; the Turk let loose a horde of irregular soldiery upon

By kind permission of the Proprietors of "Punch"

EMPRESS AND EARL;

OR, ONE GOOD TURN DESERVES ANOTHER

LORD BEACONSFIELD—"Thanks, your Majesty! I might have had it before! *Now* I think I have *earned* it."

the half-armed peasants, and the atrocities, with the news of which all Europe rang, were the result. The Queen, vividly recalling the events preceding the Crimean War, and anxious now, as then and always, to preserve the peace of Europe, was horrified at the news of the atrocities. She urged Lord Derby, then at the Foreign Office, to make it clear that England was as anxious as any other Power to promote an "amelioration of the condition of all classes and sects in Turkey" and had "no intention of making the State of the Ottoman Empire a cause of quarrel with Russia." Four months later (October 17, 1876) the Queen had evidently become more suspicious of Russia, who, "under the pretext of wishing to protect the Christians in the Principalities, wishes to obtain possession of a portion of Turkey, if not of Constantinople. . . . This we could never allow!" But how prevent it? "It seems to me," wrote the Queen in an interesting memorandum,[1] "that the great object in view ought to be to remove from Russia the *pretext* for constantly threatening the peace of Europe on the Eastern question. The only way to do this seems to me to "free the Principalities from Turkish rule and to unite them under an independent Prince to make that Principality a neutral State."

Meanwhile, the crisis had, as the next chapter will show, drawn Mr. Gladstone out of his retirement. He called upon Christian Europe to expel the unspeakable Turk.

Russia took the task of expulsion into her own hands. Her armies, though held up at Plevna, reached Adrianople in January 1878, and the Czar dictated to the Sultan the terms of the Treaty of San Stefano which virtually extinguished the Ottoman Empire in Europe.

Down to this point the British Government, though, like the Queen, they were rendered increasingly anxious by the

[1] *Q.V.L.*, II, II, 488.

advance of Russia, had maintained strict neutrality. Telegrams and letters from the Queen now descended in torrents on the heads of Ministers. She formally appealed to the Cabinet to show "a bold and united front to the enemy in the country as well as outside it," while to the Prime Minister she wrote that "if England is to kiss Russia's feet, she will not be a party to the humiliation of England, and would lay down her Crown."

The Treaty of San Stefano brought matters to a crisis. The British Government demanded that the treaty should, in its entirety, be submitted to a European Congress. But there were divisions in the Cabinet. When it decided to ask for a vote of £6,000,000 and to send the Fleet to the Dardanelles, Lord Carnarvon and Lord Derby threatened to resign. "Let Lord Derby and Lord Carnarvon go," wrote the Queen to Lord Beaconsfield, " and be *very firm*. A divided Cabinet is of NO *use*." At the same time she offered him the Garter, which he declined. Lord Carnarvon retired in February, and Lord Derby (finally) in March. The Queen was anxious to secure Lord Lyons for the Foreign Office, but it was ultimately given to Lord Salisbury, while Sir Michael Hicks-Beach, of whom Lord Beaconsfield had a high opinion, went to the Colonial Office. On April 17 it was announced that 7,000 Indian troops had been ordered to embark for Malta; Austria supported the demand of England for a European Congress; Bismarck was behind Austria, and in June the Congress assembled under his presidency at Berlin.

England and Russia had already agreed on terms. So long as Russia retained Batoum and Kars, England was to occupy and administer the island of Cyprus.

Lord Beaconsfield and Lord Salisbury brought back "Peace with Honour" from Berlin, and were welcomed with tumultuous enthusiasm.

That was the zenith of Lord Beaconsfield's career, and an eminently characteristic one. No wonder he was "in high spirits" when the Queen (July 20) received him at Osborne. Her welcome to her Minister is described as "almost rapturous." She gave him the Garter, and (at his suggestion) to Lord Salisbury also. But "would he not accept a Marquisate or Dukedom *in addition* to the Blue Ribbon? And will he not allow the Queen to settle a Barony or Viscounty on his Brother and Nephew? Such a name should be perpetuated!" But though he accepted the Garter he thought he was "ennobled thro' your Majesty's goodness quite enough. . . . The belief that your Majesty trusts and approves of him is more precious than rubies." The man was absolutely sincere.

The belief persists, that if Lord Beaconsfield had dissolved Parliament on his return from Berlin, the country would have given him a large majority. It is impossible to say. London had given him an enthusiastic welcome; but London is not England. Anyway, the next two years formed a deplorable anti-climax: harvests failed; trade was depressed; banks closed their doors; distress was general.

Further afield things were no better. The "forward" policy pursued by Lord Lytton involved us in disaster in Afghanistan; in South Africa a series of disputes with the Zulus led in January 1879 to the outbreak of war. In the course of that war, marked by a grievous disaster at Isandhlwana and the heroic defence of Rorke's Drift, the young Prince Imperial lost his life. The Queen was greatly distressed by the death of "such an amiable, good young man who would have made such a good Emperor for France one day," and did everything in her power to comfort the bereaved Empress Eugénie. She went to Chislehurst to bear the Empress company during the Prince's funeral, and when (in 1880) the House of Commons refused—very

properly—to erect a monument in the Abbey, she consoled herself by putting one in St. George's, Windsor, "a fitter and safer place for this monument."

On every side the closing years of Lord Beaconsfield's Government were marked by distress and disaster. But three by-elections in the winter of 1879–80—at Sheffield, Liverpool, and in London, where Mr. (afterwards Sir Edward) Clarke won a sensational victory—went so well for the Government that the Cabinet was tempted to ask for a Dissolution in March, instead of waiting until the autumn.

The Prime Minister's election manifesto took the form of a letter to the Duke of Marlborough, Lord-Lieutenant of Ireland, in which he called attention to the Separatist agitation in that country, and appealed to the electorate to defeat it and so affirm the "imperial character of this realm."

Meanwhile, Mr. Gladstone had been conducting a vigorous campaign in Midlothian, directed primarily against the fustian Imperialism of his detested rival. Mr. Gladstone prevailed. His campaign gave the Liberals in 1880 a majority of nearly 120 over the Conservatives, of 50 over Conservatives and Home Rulers combined. The Queen was "greatly distressed," regarding the result ("Liberal as she has ever been but never Radical or democratic") as "a great calamity for the country and the peace of Europe."

On Lord Beaconsfield's resignation the Queen applied to Lord Hartington and to Lord Granville as leaders of the Liberal Party. This was strictly in accord with constitutional conventions; but neither would undertake the formation of a Government. Most reluctantly, therefore, the Queen was persuaded to send for Mr. Gladstone, who for the second time took office as Prime Minister.

The Queen was desolated at the loss of Lord Beaconsfield's political services; but she was determined to retain him as a friend, and to seek from him solace if not counsel. He, meanwhile, solaced himself by writing *Endymion*, and by maintaining a fairly regular correspondence with the Queen. In the early spring of 1881, however, he became seriously ill, and on April 19, to the great grief of his Mistress, he passed away. To Lord Granville the Queen confessed that she was "overwhelmed with the loss of one of the kindest, truest, and best friends and wisest counsellors she ever had." Nor did she conceal her grief from Mr. Gladstone, who, while not "dissembling the amount and character of the separation between Lord Beaconsfield and himself," tactfully confessed himself to be "well aware of his own marked inferiority" and anxiously desirous "to profit by a great example."

In Lord Beaconsfield's wish to be buried, not in the Abbey, but by his wife's side at Hughenden, the Queen cordially acquiesced. There on April 26 he was laid to rest with the simplicity he desired. But the Prince of Wales, the Duke of Connaught and Prince Leopold (representing the Queen) attended the funeral; and besides most of his old colleagues there were also present Lord Rosebery, Lord Hartington and Sir William Harcourt. On the flower-covered coffin were two wreaths from the Queen, one entirely of primroses, with an inscription, "His favourite flowers from Osborne, a tribute of affection from Queen Victoria." Four days later the Queen drove over from Windsor and placed on his coffin, in the reopened vault, a wreath of China flowers. Later on, she erected, at her private expense, a monument to his memory in the chancel of Hughenden Church. It bore the inscription: "To the dear and honoured memory of Benjamin, Earl of Beaconsfield, this memorial is placed by his grateful Sovereign and Friend, Victoria R.I.

'Kings love him that speaketh right' (Proverbs xvi. 13). February 27, 1882."

The monument recalls a relationship between Sovereign and Statesman which was, and will probably remain, unique. What other Prime Minister was ever addressed by his Sovereign as "Dearest Lord——"; to what other did the Queen subscribe herself as "Ever yours affectionately, V.R. and I."? [1]

[1] See Buckle: *Life*, VI, 614, and *Q.V.L.*, II, III, 128 and 144.

J. E. Millais pinx. *T. O. Barlow sc.*

WILLIAM EWART GLADSTONE

CHAPTER IX

MR. GLADSTONE—THE ADVENT OF DEMOCRACY

CONTRASTS and comparisons seem, in certain cases, so inevitable as to be part of the order of nature. One school of historians found it impossible to appreciate Canning without attacking Castlereagh. To few critics in the Victorian era was it given to detect genius alike in *Vanity Fair* and *David Copperfield.* Similarly, historical commentators apparently find it difficult to do justice both to Disraeli and Gladstone.[1] To avoid comparison in this case is, indeed, impossible. The two men towered above all their fellows; for a full generation they confronted each other nightly in the House of Commons; they were congenitally antipathetic, and in training and in tradition, as in their outlook upon men and things, they were widely apart. Yet they entered public life in company. Gladstone was, indeed, recognized as the "rising hope of the stern, unbending Tories" at a time when Disraeli was regarded as a mere adventurer with

[1] Gladstone, William Ewart, b. 1809; ed. Eton and Christ Church; M.P. (Conservative) for Newark (1832, 1835, 1837, 1841–5); Junior Lord of Treasury (1834); Under-Secretary for Colonies (1835); Vice-President Board of Trade (1841); President (1843); Colonial Secretary (1845–6); M.P. for Oxford University (Peelite) (1847–65); Chancellor of Exchequer (1852–5); Special Commissioner to Ionian Isles (1858–9); Chancellor of Exchequer (1859–65); M.P. South Lancashire (1865–8); Leader H. of C. and Chancellor of Exchequer (1865–6); Leader Liberal Party (1867); P.M. (1868–74; 1880–5; 1886; 1892–4); Chancellor of Exchequer (1880–2); M.P. Greenwich (1868–80); M.P. Midlothian (1880–95); d. May 19, 1898; buried in Westminster Abbey.

some literary reputation and a leaning towards socialism but with no political prospects. Gladstone, like Peel, belonged to the new commercial aristocracy, and started life with all the advantages of inherited wealth, and of friendships made at Eton and Christ Church. To his friendship with the son of the Duke of Newcastle he owed his nomination for the pocket-borough of Newark and his entrance into the House of Commons at the age of twenty-three. Disraeli was ten years older when, after several unsuccessful attempts to enter Parliament, he at last found a seat through the favour of Mrs. Wyndham Lewis, who became, later on, his devoted helpmeet. Gladstone's success was from the outset assured, and before he left Oxford he was "spotted" as a future Prime Minister. Only Disraeli himself had any premonition of his ultimate triumph; and, as we have seen, he was an old man before (in his own phrase) he had "climbed to the top of the greasy pole."

Gladstone, in later life, recalled the fact that he had been "brought up under the shadow of the great name of Mr. Canning." Liverpool, Canning's constituency and Gladstone's birthplace, common membership of the Eton Society ("Pop"), and their parallel careers at Oxford, contributed, doubtless, to Gladstone's retrospective conviction. But, in fact, his early Toryism was of a much more romantic hue than Canning's or Pitt's. His creed was inspired by Filmer rather than by Bolingbroke. All the more violent, therefore, was the subsequent rebound; but it was not until after he was "unmuzzled" by the action of the Oxford graduates (1865) that his liberalism became manifestly "advanced." In 1858 Disraeli was prepared to make way for him as Conservative leader in the House of Commons; he remained a member of the Carlton Club until 1866, and as late as 1865 he opposed Mr. Goschen's Bill for the abolition of Tests at the Universities, and refused to accept

Dillwyn's motion declaring the state of the Irish Church to be "unsatisfactory." Moreover, although his career as Prime Minister synchronized with the advent of Democracy, Gladstone himself was more of a demagogue than a democrat. In some respects, indeed, the man who had opposed the Reform Bill of 1832 remained to the end of his long life a Tory.

A staunch believer in the Divine origin of the Church, he had a profound respect for Monarchy as an institution, and consistently laboured to shield from criticism the actual occupant of the throne.

Yet the relations between the Queen and Mr. Gladstone were, in later years at any rate, strained almost to the breaking-point. A few years ago Mr. Herbert (Viscount) Gladstone proved his filial devotion and his Radical partisanship by a bitter attack upon the policy of Lord Beaconsfield, and by severe strictures upon the editor of the later volumes of Queen Victoria's *Letters*, if not upon the conduct of the Queen herself. He was more particularly concerned to show that up to 1876 Mr. Gladstone's [1] relations with the Queen were "good and friendly." In this endeavour he was not wholly unsuccessful; but he conspicuously failed to prove that the Queen's "newborn dislike of Mr. Gladstone" was due to the malign influence of Lord Beaconsfield.

It is, however, indisputable that until after he had become her First Minister the Queen betrayed no dislike of Mr. Gladstone. Why should she? If Mr. Gladstone was brought up "under the shadow of the great name of Mr. Canning," he became, early in his ministerial career, the ardent disciple of the Queen's favourite Minister, Sir Robert Peel. Still more had Gladstone commended himself to the Queen by his admiration, frequently expressed, for the Prince Consort,

[1] *After Thirty Years* (Macmillan & Co., 1928).

and by the sympathy which he showed to the Queen in her bereavement. "Of all her Ministers," wrote a mutual friend to Gladstone, "she seemed to me to think that you had entered most into her feelings." Soon after the Prince's death Gladstone was summoned to Windsor and had a long interview with the Queen, who received him "with great kindness." "All was beautiful, noble, touching to the very last degree." So he wrote to the Duchess of Sutherland, and in a memorandum recorded his impressions: "I was astonished at her humility . . . I never was more struck with the firm texture and elasticity of her mind, and her marked dignity and strength of character. I came away from her . . . with heightened interest and admiration." Then again: Gladstone shared with the Queen a profound mistrust of Palmerston, and the correspondence between those ill-assorted colleagues, especially during the years 1859 and 1865, reveals a constant divergence of opinion between the Prime Minister and his Chancellor of the Exchequer. More than once Palmerston was constrained to rebuke Gladstone, though in the most good-humoured way, for having broken by his speeches, both in and out of Parliament, the convention about Cabinet solidarity. Thus in April 1862 Palmerston wrote: "When fourteen or fifteen men are brought together to deliberate upon a course of action, it is scarcely possible that all should take exactly the same view of the matter discussed, but some decision or other must be come to, and those who have yielded their own opinion, even if they have not been convinced, do not, when the decision of the Body is acted upon, proclaim to the world their dissent from the course pursued."

The rebuke was well deserved; nor was anyone more insistent than Mr. Gladstone himself, after he became Prime Minister, on the doctrine of Cabinet solidarity. "While each Minister," he wrote, "is an adviser of the Crown, the Cabinet is a unity, and none of its members can advise as an individual without, or in opposition to, his colleagues."[1]

At the General Election of 1865, Mr. Gladstone, having been defeated at Oxford, was for the first time elected to represent a great popular constituency, South Lancashire. Three months later Lord Palmerston died, Lord Russell retired from public life in 1867, and Gladstone succeeded him as leader of the Liberal Party. In the same year Disraeli carried a Reform Bill, based on the principle (for the urban constituencies) of household suffrage. These events decided the political future of Gladstone. When, in 1868, Disraeli, having appealed unsuccessfully to the new electorate, resigned office, the Queen sent without hesitation for his rival.

Gladstone's first Ministry included a large proportion of men who, like himself, belonged to the "new aristocracy" of commerce and intellect. Lord Hartington, Lord Clarendon (who returned to the Foreign Office), Lord Kimberley, the Duke of Argyll and others represented the class which had governed England with eminent success for two centuries. But side by side with them were men who, though highly educated and conspicuously able, had no hereditary claims to office. Prominent among them were Edward Cardwell, perhaps the greatest of army reformers; Robert Lowe, who, despite his great abilities, found himself ill-placed at the Treasury; Hugh Childers, at the Admiralty, where he was presently succeeded by Mr. Goschen; John Bright, and William Edward Forster, a Bradford manufacturer, whose Education Bill made history. No previous Cabinet, with the possible exception of Lord Aberdeen's, had contained so many men of outstanding ability. Yet, by common consent, the Prime Minister stood alone.

For twenty years—ever since the defeat of Peel in 1846

[1] *Gleanings*, I, 242.

—Gladstone's position in Parliament had been uneasy and ambiguous. The Peelites were "staff officers without any army." Individually they lent strength to any Ministry they could be persuaded to join. But the House of Commons is no place for a leader without followers. Even a private member, if he desires to be effective, must speak on behalf of a group, or represent an interest. Isolation, save in very exceptional cases, is fatal to parliamentary success. By the Budgets of 1853 and 1854, and by the long and unbroken series for which he was responsible between 1859 and 1866, Gladstone had established his reputation as the greatest financier of that or any other age. But until the removal of Palmerston from the scene Gladstone was restless, and his political future was uncertain. From 1868 onwards he was a new man; until 1885 his hold upon his Party was undisputed, and of the new governing class—the middle-class Dissenters—he was the idol. But he had still to establish, curiously enough, his position in the House of Commons. The Queen and the Prince Consort had formed a high opinion of his abilities and character, and in 1852 urged Lord Derby to give him the leadership of the House in preference either to Palmerston or Disraeli. Derby's reply may have argued a lack of acumen, but it represented a prevalent opinion. Mr. Gladstone, he said, was "quite unfit to lead the House of Commons; he had none of that decision, boldness, readiness and clearness which was necessary to lead a Party, to inspire it with confidence, and still more to take a decision on the spur of the moment which a leader had often to do." In view of Gladstone's position during his first two administrations, these words read strangely. Yet Lord Derby was not entirely mistaken. As a parliamentary leader Gladstone was not in the same class with Walpole, the younger Pitt, or Disraeli. His strength rested on the confidence of the Electorate; so long as the

Electorate gave him a large parliamentary majority he could, with the aid of his matchless eloquence, *overawe* the House of Commons, but he never *led* it, as did Pitt, while as the leader of an opposition he was curiously ineffective.

The Parliament of 1868–74 was mainly occupied with Irish questions, with the rejection and subsequent enactment of the Ballot Bill, and with elementary education. In foreign affairs interest centred on the Franco-German War and its *sequelæ*, and on the settlement of the *Alabama* claims. About the Ballot Bill, the Queen was not much concerned, nor about the Education Act. Between her and its sponsor, however, a real friendship sprang up. Soon after the passing of his Bill, Forster went for the first time to Balmoral as Minister in Attendance. He conceived for the Queen a deep and loyal devotion, while she was greatly attracted by his simplicity and straightforwardness. When he resigned with the Government in 1874, the Queen addressed to him a shrewd and kindly warning as to his future conduct in opposition,[1] and after his death (1886) she wrote a touching letter to his widow expressing her "true and sincere concern . . . at the loss of one . . . who served his Queen and country, bravely, truly and loyally." "We can ill afford," she wrote, "to lose so honest, so unselfish and so courageous a statesman. . . ." Then, as always, the Queen was specially concerned with foreign policy; it was, therefore, the more unfortunate that of all the appointments in the new Ministry, the only one to which she took serious objection was Lord Clarendon's as Foreign Secretary. Critical opinion assigns to Clarendon a high place among the Foreign Ministers of the reign, but for reasons never satisfactorily explained the Queen disliked him. She complained to General Grey that "he was the only one of her Ministers who had ever been impertinent to her." Perhaps

[1] *Q.V.L.*, II, II, 315.

she was aware that he habitually spoke of her as "Eliza," a habit which, apart from other objections, offended her as being faintly reminiscent of the Tudor Queen whom she detested. Anyway, she was annoyed by his reappointment to a post for which she would in 1868 have preferred Lord Granville, who succeeded to it on Clarendon's death (1870). Clarendon would seem, before then, to have mended his ways, for the Queen, though describing him as "very satirical . . . irritable and hasty," appreciated his ability and deplored his death. In the Ministry of '80 Lord Granville entirely forfeited the Queen's earlier esteem.

Still more did his Chief. It was not until his second Ministry that relations between the Sovereign and Gladstone were definitely strained. For the Monarchy as an institution the Radical leader had an immense veneration. For the Queen herself he had conceived an admiration not unmingled with affection. The warm tribute he paid to the Queen's attitude during the Schleswig-Holstein crisis has been already quoted.

Even more warmly did he acknowledge the debt which he owed to the Queen for smoothing the passage of his Irish Church Bill. The Queen had no sympathy with that, or any other item, in Gladstone's Irish policy. The Church, like the Monarchy and the Army, was a part of the Established Order, which it was her first duty to maintain. But she understood her position as a "constitutional" Sovereign; she was loyal to her Ministers, so long as they did not actually betray the highest interests of the country; she realized that the House of Commons in passing the Bill by large majorities reflected the sentiments, recently declared, of the constituencies; above all, she was anxious to avert a collision between the two Houses. Mr. Gladstone had written her an "explanation" of the Bill covering a dozen closely written quarto pages. She found the "explanation" more difficult to understand even than the Bill itself, and asked Mr. Theodore Martin to make a *précis* of it. But little as she liked the measure, or understood Gladstone's exposition of it, she exerted her influence with the Peers, notably with Archbishop Tait and his episcopal brethren, to allow it, with one important amendment, to become law.

Gladstone was unfeignedly grateful, and strove in vain to express to the Queen "his relief, thankfulness and satisfaction," not least for "the undoubted signal blessing of an escape from a formidable constitutional conflict."

Fifteen years later a parallel situation arose in connection with the Franchise and Redistribution Bills (1884–5). Once again the Queen was called upon to play the part of mediator between a Gladstone Government supported by the House of Commons and the recalcitrant Peers. By this time any feeling of cordiality between the Sovereign and her First Minister had entirely evaporated. But the Queen perceived that the case was one for compromise, and succeeded in bringing about direct negotiations between Mr. Gladstone and Lord Salisbury and Sir Stafford Northcote. Compromise was reached, and Mr. Gladstone again tendered his grateful thanks to the Queen for "the wise, gracious and steady influence . . . which has so powerfully contributed to bring about this accommodation, and to avert a serious crisis of affairs."

It was not, then, in relation to domestic politics, but to foreign affairs that the real breach occurred between the Queen and the Prime Minister. The Queen's attention to foreign affairs was never for an instant diverted. It needed the tyranny of a Neapolitan Bourbon or an Ottoman Sultan to compel Gladstone's attention to that department of public affairs. But in the summer of 1870 the dangerous situation on the Continent could not be ignored. The Queen's supreme anxiety, then as always, was to avert war.

But Bismarck having absorbed Schleswig-Holstein, having expelled Austria both from Germany and Italy, was bent on humbling France, and recovering for Germany Alsace and Lorraine. Napoleon III gave him an excuse, and on August 2, 1870, the war began. The British Government was determined to maintain absolute neutrality, but public opinion was at first decidedly hostile to France, who was regarded (with scant justice, as we now know) as the wanton disturber of European peace. English feelings had been deeply stirred by the publication in *The Times* (July 25) of a draft Treaty which was said to have been submitted, on behalf of France, to Bismarck in 1867. The draft virtually provided for the absorption of Belgium by France. The Emperor Napoleon declared from his camp at Metz that it was Bismarck who had offered him Belgium and that he had refused it. Whether he had ever had the chance of refusing it is doubtful; but it is certain that his account of the matter was nearer the truth than Bismarck's. Belgium was merely a pawn in Bismarck's game, the object of which was the diplomatic isolation of France. To mention Belgium was, as he well knew, to touch England on the raw. The publication in *The Times* aroused English sentiment against France, though after the fall of the Empire opinion veered round in favour of the defeated combatant. Nevertheless, the Government observed strict neutrality and for doing so incurred the bitter hostility of both parties. With the King and Queen of Prussia, as with the unhappy Empress of the French, the Queen maintained most friendly relations throughout the war, and when the German victory was assured she strongly urged the Prussian King to treat France with magnanimity. On the crucial question of Alsace-Lorraine, Gladstone was anxious that the wishes of the inhabitants should be ascertained and respected. But he got little support even in his own Cabinet. His colleagues rightly insisted that the suggestion would be interpreted in Germany as a departure from neutrality in favour of France.

The British Government did, indeed, respond to an appeal from France to obtain for her some reduction in the amount of the war indemnity; and successfully. Otherwise, we did not and could not interfere. Meanwhile, we ourselves suffered a serious diplomatic defeat. Russia, in October 1870, denounced those clauses of the Treaty of Paris (1856) which secured the neutralization of the Black Sea and inhibited both Russia and Turkey from maintaining on its coasts any military-maritime arsenals. Russia had long chafed under this restriction, and it was certain that she would take the first opportunity of getting rid of it. Bismarck presented her with an opportunity in 1870. Great Britain insisted, however, that no portion of the Treaty should be abrogated by the discretion of a single Power, that the question should be submitted to a Conference.

The Conference met in London in December 1870. The principle on which we insisted was solemnly affirmed; for the rest, Russia got all she wanted.

Not less disquieting to English pride was the award given by the arbitrators at Geneva about the *Alabama* and other claims preferred by the United States in reference to certain incidents in the Civil War. On all counts the award went against Great Britain, who was mulcted in damages to the amount of about £3,250,000. It was a "good deal cheaper than war," was the grim comment of Mr. Lowe. Gladstone remained of opinion that the sentence was unjust, but regarded "the fine imposed on this country as dust in the balance compared with the moral value of the example set when these two great nations . . . went before a judicial tribunal rather than resort to the arbitrament of war." These exalted sentiments were loudly applauded, but there was an uneasy feeling that too many of the kicks fell to our share, and the Ministry did not gain in popularity.

Closely connected with foreign affairs, and of no less concern to the Queen, were the army reforms effected by Mr. Cardwell. Among these, the one which touched the Queen most nearly was the subordination of the Commander in-Chief to the Secretary of State. The Queen always regarded herself as, in a special sense, head of the Army, and claimed to control it through the Commander-in-Chief, her cousin George, Duke of Cambridge. That he should be subordinated to a Minister responsible to Parliament was exceedingly distasteful to the Queen, but, largely in order to avert another conflict between the two Houses, she signed, though with extreme reluctance, an Order-in-Council (June 28, 1870) effecting the change. In the next year she consented, with equal reluctance and from a similar motive, to exercise the Royal Prerogative in order to abolish promotion by purchase.

In Gladstone's second Administration Mr. Childers replaced Mr. Cardwell at the War Office; but he proved no more deferential to the Queen's wishes, and it was a relief to her when he was in turn succeeded (1882) by Lord Hartington. Unfortunately, Lord Hartington's tenure of the office coincided with the Rebellion in the Sudan and the subsequent tragedy at Khartoum. For that disastrous episode the chief blame was imputed to Gladstone, and though he was destined to form two more Ministries, he never regained the place he had once held in the affections of the country. The Queen's confidence he had long since forfeited. To return to 1874. Shortly after his defeat at the General Election of 1874, Gladstone resolved to retire from the leadership of his Party. He communicated his intention to the Queen, who replied not ungraciously. "She knows that his zeal and untiring energy have always been exerted with the desire of advancing the welfare of the nation and maintaining the honour of the Crown, and she thanks him for his loyal assurances of support on all occasions when it may become necessary."

Gladstone's retirement was due—so at least he convinced himself—partly to acute divisions in his party, partly to his deep desire for "an interval between parliament and the grave," and above all to his belief that "the welfare of mankind does not now depend on the state or the world of politics."

On the last point he was quickly undeceived. He retired in February 1875. In July an insurrection broke out in Herzegovina, destined not only to reopen the whole Eastern Question, but to bring Gladstone back to active political life. Thus the desired interval between parliament and the grave was, in fact, largely filled up with increasing political activity.

The Crimean War had definitely frustrated the ambition of Russia, but had provided no permanent solution of the many problems connected with Turkish rule in Europe. Between 1856 and 1876 there was, indeed, continuous unrest in the Balkan Peninsula. In 1859 Europe recognized the union of Moldavia and Wallachia under the title of Roumania. In 1862 the Greeks expelled King Otho and tried to obtain in his place the services of an English prince, or even an English statesman. A Danish prince (King George I) eventually accepted the uneasy throne, and received the Ionian Isles from Great Britain as a christening present. Crete was only kept quiet (1866–8) by the intervention of the Powers. In 1875 the southern Slavs in Bosnia and Herzegovina broke into revolt. How far the insurrection was spontaneous, how far it was stimulated from St. Petersburg, is a question which must not now detain us.[1]

[1] Marriott, *The Eastern Question* (Clarendon Press, 3rd edition), c. xii.

The insurrection spread to Serbia and Montenegro, and later to Bulgaria. In the summer of 1876 the English people learnt with horror of the atrocities committed by the Turk in suppressing the Bulgarian insurrection. Disraeli, indeed, described the stories as "Coffee-house babble," but their substantial accuracy was very soon confirmed by the Report of Mr. Walter Baring, Second Secretary of Legation at Constantinople, who had been sent to investigate the matter on the spot.

Mr. Gladstone's feelings were deeply stirred, and in September 1876 he published his famous pamphlet, *The Bulgarian Horrors and the Question of the East.* It was circulated by tens of thousands, and its author was irresistibly dragged forth from retirement to resume his place in the forefront of the political arena. He vehemently demanded that the "Turks should be cleared out 'bag and baggage' from the province they have desolated and profaned," and hardly less vehemently that the pro-Turkish Tories with Disraeli at their head should be deprived of the power which they had so grossly abused.

Throughout the whole of 1877 he carried on his campaign with comparative moderation in the House of Commons, where Liberals were divided, but with immense vigour in the country, where he aroused the utmost enthusiasm in his party.

Throughout the whole of the crisis that ensued[1] Lord Beaconsfield enjoyed, despite the defection of Lord Derby and Lord Carnarvon, the solid support of his party. Mr. Gladstone did not. Still less could the latter command the sympathy of the Queen.

The Queen's insistence upon a vigorous policy in the Near East seemed at times to suggest that her Ministers were supine or dilatory. Both the Queen and her

[1] See *supra*, p. 136 f.

Ministers have, in fact, been severely censured for "pro-Turkish" sympathies. But in defence of their attitude during the critical months (January–June 1878), one or two observations may be made. The most important is that the vigorous preparations for war undoubtedly preserved the peace of Europe. The "pacific" Aberdeen drifted into the Crimean War because the Czar Nicholas was confident that, under no circumstances, would England draw the sword against him. The Queen, whose detestation of war was at least as strong as Aberdeen's, was determined that the Crimean blunder should not be repeated. Gladstone, who was a member of the Aberdeen Cabinet, and always frankly accepted responsibility for the war, appeared in 1878 to have forgotten it. His son declared with a dogmatic finality: "Lord Beaconsfield's Eastern policy was wrong and broke down. Mr. Gladstone's was right, and it prevailed. For the one a pinnacle. For the other the depths of royal disfavour." [1]

Against authority so pontifical it were vain to argue: but it is permissible to remark that Lord Beaconsfield obtained by peaceful Treaty at Berlin what Mr. Gladstone and his colleagues had failed to secure by the Crimean War. The only effective barrier to Russian aggression in South-Eastern Europe, the only basis for a permanent solution of the Balkan problem, is to revive and sustain the national spirit of the indigenous peoples of the peninsula. The Treaty of San Stefano would have made Russia supreme in the Balkans: the Treaty of Berlin kept open the door to the revival of nationalism. Through that door Jugo-Slavia, Roumania, Bulgaria and Greece have emerged to take their place as independent Sovereign States in the European polity, to supersede the Turk, and to bar Russia's path to Constantinople.

It is vain to inquire what would or might have happened

[1] *After Thirty Years*, p. xvi.

had the "right" policy of Gladstone really prevailed, and had he ousted Lord Beaconsfield from power in 1877; but it is pertinent to insist that there may have been reasons, quite other than those suggested by the filial piety of Viscount Gladstone, for the Queen's profound mistrust of his father, and for the confidence which she reposed in his rival.

The mistrust aroused in the Queen's mind by Gladstone's conduct in opposition (1876–80) was not dissipated when he returned to office in 1880. Was her reluctance to accept him as First Minister due entirely, as his son has maintained, to the malign influence of the Queen's new favourite? That she did everything to avoid the disagreeable necessity that faced her is a matter of history. But she was well within her constitutional rights in approaching the recognized leaders of the Liberal Party in both Houses before sending for a statesman who had ostentatiously retired from leadership. She would have transgressed conventions had she done otherwise. But the General Election of 1880 was in effect a plebiscite for Mr. Gladstone, and Lord Hartington and Lord Granville were alike emphatic in advising her to recognize the fact.

Small wonder that the Queen's reception of a Minister thus forced upon her by the Electorate should have been something less than cordial. Nevertheless, Mr. Gladstone was deeply pained, and in his Diary (July 16, 1881) records, after an audience with the Queen: "She is as ever perfect in her courtesy, but as to confidence she holds me now at arm's length." And again (Nov. 30): "Much civility . . . but I am always outside an iron ring, and without any desire had I the power to break it through."

From the Queen's point of view, as from that of the nation, things went steadily from bad to worse during the five years that ensued on Gladstone's return to power. The

House of Commons was perpetually distracted, its business interrupted and its prestige lowered by the Bradlaugh controversy—the claim of a professed atheist returned by Northampton, as the colleague of Mr. Labouchere, to make an affirmation instead of taking the customary oath, and subsequently to take an oath in the sanctity of which he avowedly disbelieved.

This was the least of the troubles that confronted the new Government. India, South Africa and Ireland all presented problems difficult of solution; and in no case did the Queen approve of the solution which commended itself to her Ministers. Kandahar, the fruit of General Roberts's brilliant victory, was restored to the Amir of Afghanistan, despite the strong protest of the Queen, who agreed with Roberts that its retention was "of vital importance." The rendition of Kandahar meant the reversal of Lord Lytton's "Forward" policy on the north-west frontier.

A similar principle governed Gladstone's policy in South Africa. In 1887 Sir Theophilus Shepstone, acting on a discretion allowed him by Lord Carnarvon, had annexed the Transvaal to the British Crown. The annexation saved the Boers of the Transvaal from destruction at the hands of the Zulus. In the Zulu War (1879) we finally dissipated that danger. The Boers, saved from their enemies, demanded their country back. Mr. Gladstone handed it back, but not until after the Boers had inflicted a series of defeats, culminating in the disaster of Majuba Hill, upon a small force which had been sent to maintain British authority. The Queen regarded the rendition as a humiliating surrender, and her feelings were largely shared both by this country and by the loyalists in South Africa.

Ireland presented problems even more difficult and insistent than South Africa and Afghanistan. Immediate responsibility for Irish policy rested on Mr. W. E. Forster, who became Chief Secretary with a seat in the Cabinet, and Lord Cowper, who was Viceroy without one. But in this, as in all other departments, Gladstone's will was dominant. His policy was an amalgam of conciliation and coercion. Conciliation was offered mainly at the expense of the Irish landlords. That the land system in Ireland called urgently for reform is undeniable: but had Mr. Gladstone (who had little personal acquaintance with Ireland) listened to the advice of the wiser men in his own party—notably Mr. Bright (who knew Ireland well), reform would have proceeded, not upon the lines of the Land Act of 1881, but on those subsequently followed by Lord Ashbourne and Mr. Wyndham. Dual ownership created by the Act of 1881 could only lead to future trouble. The true policy was to enable the tenants, with the aid of State credit, to purchase their holdings and become the owners of the soil. That object was attained by the Conservative legislation of 1885 and 1903. The Land Act of 1881 cost Gladstone one of his ablest colleagues, the Duke of Argyll, who refused to support the Bill. His administrative vacillation cost him two Chief Secretaries. Mr. Forster had waged a brave fight against lawlessness in Ireland, but resigned in 1882, refusing to be a party to the pact with Parnell, known as the Kilmainham Treaty (from the gaol in which Parnell and his colleagues had been incarcerated). Lord Frederick Cavendish, who succeeded Forster, was stabbed to death with his under-secretary, Mr. Burke, in Phœnix Park, before he could take up his difficult task. The Queen was moved to mingled grief and indignation by "this awful, appalling catastrophe," and did not hesitate to attribute responsibility to Mr. Gladstone and "his violent Radical advisers." To Gladstone himself, whom she knew to be "stunned and overwhelmed by the terrible blow which has shocked all the world," she wrote in terms not devoid of consideration, but to Lord

Granville, who was at this time the chief intermediary between herself and the Cabinet, she made no secret of her feelings. Such catastrophes were, she held, the natural result of encouraging lawless rebels at the expense of law-abiding citizens. She so far prevailed that increased powers were conferred upon the Executive in Ireland, the murderers of Lord Frederick and Mr. Burke were brought to justice, and by the calm, courageous and even-handed administration of Lord Spencer and Sir George Trevelyan, the agrarian crimes were gradually stamped out, and order restored.

After Ireland, Egypt. For nearly twenty years Egypt had been groaning under the "carnival of extravagance and oppression" (the apt phrase is Lord Milner's) in which its ruler, the Khedive Ismail, had indulged. In 1879 the Powers, partly in the interests of his miserable subjects, partly in those of their own bondholders, induced his suzerain, the Sultan, to depose the Khedive. His son and successor, Tewfik, though well meaning, was not strong enough to cope with a situation in itself difficult enough and further complicated in September 1881 by a successful revolt led by Arabi Bey. The condition of the country became more and more chaotic; in January 1882 England and France, representing the largest bondholders, assured Tewfik of their support, but he was powerless to restore order, and in the summer of 1882 an *émeute* at Alexandria, resulting in the slaughter of some fifty Europeans, precipitated intervention. The English and French fleets were anchored in the roads of Alexandria, but the French declined to co-operate in protecting European lives. The British fleet had to act alone; the forts of Alexandria were destroyed by gunfire, and Arabi released the convicts, marched off with his troops and delivered the city up to fire, pillage and massacre. A body of bluejackets and marines were landed and tardily restored order in a ruined city.

That was the beginning of the British occupation. An army, recruited partly from England and partly from India, was placed under the command of Sir Garnet Wolseley, who inflicted a crushing defeat on Arabi at Tel-el-Kebir and occupied Cairo. Arabi was deported, after trial, to Ceylon; on England rested the task of restoring order to a distracted country. The Powers were informed that we should remain in occupation of Egypt only so long as was necessary for its accomplishment.

But complications ensued. In 1883 the Mahdi headed a revolt in the Sudan; a wretchedly disciplined Egyptian army was sent, under a British general, Hicks Pasha, to suppress it. The general, his European staff and most of the force were killed. Sir Evelyn Baring (afterwards the Earl of Cromer), who in 1883 had been sent to Egypt as Consul-General, advised the abandonment of the Sudan. But how to withdraw the Egyptian forces blockaded in Khartoum and elsewhere? General Charles Gordon offered himself for the job; the distracted Cabinet eagerly accepted his offer; in January 1884 he was sent out; was appointed Governor-General of the Sudan by the Khedive, and soon after his arrival at Khartoum found himself besieged by the Mahdists in that city. Baring, though he had disapproved of Gordon's mission, insisted that he must be rescued. For month after month the Cabinet at home, despite the urging of the Queen, delayed action. "It is alarming; General Gordon is in danger; you are bound to try and save him . . . you have incurred fearful responsibility." So the Queen telegraphed on March 25, 1884, to Lord Hartington, then War Secretary. As the spring advanced the Queen became increasingly alarmed and insistent; the Cabinet remained immovably dilatory. "If not for humanity's sake, for the honour of the Government and the nation he (Gordon) must not be abandoned." So she telegraphed to Sir Henry Ponsonby on March 27, and added: "The Queen has no confidence in Lord Granville; he is as weak as water and she fears the influence of Lord Derby is harmful." The country concurred in her opinion of Lord Granville. Sir E. Baring came home on furlough in May and personally pressed the Government to act, but reported to the Queen that Gladstone seemed to think the matter of "secondary importance, whereas it is most vital." The whole conduct of the Government in the Egyptian business seemed to the Queen *"perfectly miserable."* Not even a bitterly worded telegram from Gordon himself could bring Gladstone to the point of decision, but a threat of resignation from Hartington did, in August, induce him to ask the House of Commons for the paltry sum of £300,000 to enable the Government to "undertake operations for the relief of General Gordon should they become necessary."

Lord Wolseley was at last despatched at the head of a relief expedition and made all possible haste. But he was too late. Khartoum fell and Gordon was killed on January 26, 1885. Two days later an advance guard of the expeditionary force came in sight of the city.

News of the tragedy reached London on February 5; the whole country was moved by grief and indignation and generally concurred with the Queen in holding Gladstone responsible. The matter has been endlessly discussed: but to little purpose. It may well be that Gordon's own temperament and conduct were partly to blame for the disaster. He was certainly a "difficult" subordinate. But the Ministry was responsible, in the first place, for employing him, and then culpably procrastinating in dealing with the crisis when it arose. Lord Hartington was blameworthy in not compelling his chief to give attention to a desperately urgent matter: but the public instinct was not at fault in fixing primary responsibility on the head of the Government. The Opposition moved a vote of censure, which was defeated only by 14 votes, but Gladstone thought that slender majority sufficient. The Government decided that the power of the Mahdi must be crushed, but on April 21 the policy was suddenly reversed, and the Sudan, despite vehement protests from the Queen, was abandoned. The decision may have been precipitated by news of a Russian advance towards Afghanistan. Parliament promptly passed a vote of credit for £11,000,000. Preparations for war were pushed on with a rapidity startling in contrast with the dilatoriness which had marked the despatch of a force to the Sudan. The Russians promptly agreed to arbitration, and the Penjdeh "incident" was closed.

But for the Gladstone Ministry the sands were running out. On June 8 a hostile amendment to the Budget was carried by a majority of 12, and on the 9th Mr. Gladstone tendered his resignation to the Queen. According to her wont, she deprecated a change of Government—even for the better, but, without definitely accepting Gladstone's resignation, sent for Lord Salisbury.

The situation was complicated.

Lord Salisbury was averse to taking office in a minority, the more so as the passing of the Franchise and Redistribution Acts on immediate dissolution was impossible. By the Franchise Act the principle of household suffrage, adopted for the Boroughs in 1867, was extended to the Counties. This meant the addition of some 2,000,000 electors to the Register, and the new Register could not be ready before November. The Redistribution Act of 1885 had divided almost the whole of Great Britain, urban and rural, into single-member constituencies. No appeal could, however, be made to them before November at earliest. Lord Salisbury was therefore in a real difficulty, but as Gladstone persisted in his resignation, Lord Salisbury, as the next chapter will explain, consented to form a Ministry.

The Queen's farewell letter to Mr. Gladstone was couched "in very civil terms." The expression is her own. Gladstone described it as a "generous, most generous letter." It contained the offer of an Earldom, which the Queen hoped he would accept "as a mark of her recognition of his long and distinguished services," and as likely to be "beneficial to his health." Mr. Gladstone, with genuine emotion, declined the offer, and (to Lord Granville) referred to the Queen's letter as one "which moves and almost upsets me. It must have cost her much to write and is really a pearl of great price." To the Queen he wrote: "It will be a precious possession to him and his children after him. All that could recommend an Earldom to him, it already has given him."

Parliament was dissolved in November. The new constituencies returned 335 Liberals as against 249 Conservatives. The Irish Home Rulers numbered 86, and by joining the Conservatives could have kept the Liberals out of power. Mr. Gladstone then announced his conversion to the principle of Home Rule; the Salisbury Ministry was defeated on an amendment to the Address by a combination of Radicals and Home Rulers and immediately resigned.

The Queen was distraught with anxiety; she besought Mr. Goschen to encourage his Whig friends to offer support to Lord Salisbury. She dreaded the return of Mr. Gladstone to power: "He will ruin the country if he can" (she wrote to Goschen), "and how much mischief has he not done already." Mr. Goschen, however, begged the Queen to excuse him from obeying a summons to Osborne lest it should further compromise a critical situation, and advised the Queen to send for Mr. Gladstone.

This, most reluctantly, she did, and Mr. Gladstone for

the third time became Prime Minister. But his Ministry revealed a deep fissure in the Liberal Party: Lord Hartington, Mr. Goschen, Mr. Forster, Mr. Bright, Lord Selborne, Lord Derby, Lord Northbrook and the Duke of Argyll were among the ex-Liberal Ministers who stood aside from the new Government. Sir Henry James, an ex-Attorney-General, refused the Woolsack, and before Mr. Gladstone introduced his Home Rule Bill, Chamberlain and Trevelyan joined the dissentient Liberals in opposition to their old chief.

On April 8, in a speech of transcendent power, Gladstone laid his Irish scheme before the House of Commons. Ireland was to have a separate Legislature with an Executive responsible thereto; she was to have power to control all purely Irish as distinct from Imperial affairs, and to be no longer represented in either House at Westminster. A Land Purchase Bill, designed to utilize the credit of the State for buying out the Irish landlords, was introduced in the following week. Both Bills encountered strong opposition, not least from Gladstone's former colleagues, and on the night of June 7th the Home Rule Bill was defeated by 343 votes to 313, the majority including 93 Liberals.

The Queen immediately granted the Dissolution for which Gladstone asked. The electorate returned no fewer than 394 members pledged to oppose Home Rule, of whom 316 were Conservatives. Consequently, Lord Salisbury, though he would have preferred to serve under Lord Hartington, again took office as Prime Minister.

The new Parliament, after a life of six years, was dissolved in June 1892, and Mr. Gladstone appealed to the country for a mandate in favour of Home Rule. It gave him a precarious majority of 40, drawn largely from the "Celtic fringe." England was still staunchly Unionist; most of the

269 Conservatives and many of the 46 Liberal Unionists were returned by English constituencies. The amendment to the Address was moved by Mr. H. H. Asquith, a young Oxonian who had entered Parliament in 1886 and quickly established a reputation for brilliant talents. It was carried by 40 votes. Lord Salisbury immediately resigned, and Gladstone, aged 82, again became Prime Minister. Lord Rosebery returned to the Foreign Office,[1] Sir Henry Campbell-Bannerman to the War Office, and Mr. Asquith became Home Secretary. The key position in the new Ministry was, however, the Irish Office, to which Mr. John Morley returned as Chief Secretary.

The session of 1893 was wholly dominated by the Irish Question. Mr. Gladstone introduced his second edition of Home Rule on February 13. It differed in important respects from the first. The Irish Parliament was to be frankly bicameral, and 40 Irish members (after an "in and out" arrangement had been dropped) were to be retained, for all purposes, at Westminster. Majorities in favour of the Bill or its clauses rarely numbered more than 40 in the House of Commons, and the Lords summarily rejected it by 419 votes to 41. The Lords accepted with amendments a Parish Councils Bill, which completed the new edifice of Local Government begun in 1888 by the Conservatives, but rejected an Employers Liability Bill.

Mr. Gladstone, with the ardour of 84, wanted to dissolve Parliament immediately and launch a campaign in the country against the House of Lords, but Asquith records that all his colleagues agreed in condemning that course as "madness." To the end of his life, however, Gladstone remained unconvinced, and in his last conversation with Morley (1897) maintained that his colleagues had made a grievous blunder.

[1] See *infra*, p. 176.

They had, in fact, come reluctantly to the conclusion that now was "the appointed hour for their chief's resignation." He was 84; he was very deaf and nearly blind, and was, moreover, hopelessly at issue with the great majority of his Cabinet on the question of Naval Expenditure, which (with Harcourt) he wished further to reduce. He remained "immovable as Gibraltar": but on March 1 he presided for the last time over what he described, with some contempt for the emotion they naturally displayed, as the "blubbering Cabinet."

"Resigned! I did not resign—I was put out." So the intrepid old warrior was wont to declare. On the same day he made his last speech in the House, which he had first addressed sixty-one years before. The speech was a declaration of war on the House of Lords.

On March 3 he had his last audience of the Queen at Windsor and tendered his formal resignation, which was promptly accepted. The Queen expressed her regret for the "cause" ("somewhat emphasized," Mr. Gladstone thought), but the conversation between them was brief and "negative. There was not one syllable on the past: except a repetition, an emphatic repetition of the thanks she had long ago rendered for what I had done . . . in the matter of the Duke of Coburg. . . . There is in all this a great sincerity"—so Mr. Gladstone himself records. The Queen's own account of the audience is brief and colourless, but of her farewell interview with Mrs. Gladstone she writes in her *Journal*: "She was very much upset, poor thing, and asked to be allowed to speak, as her husband 'could not speak.' This was to say, which she did with many tears, that whatever his errors might have been 'his devotion to your Majesty and the Crown were very great.' She repeated this twice, and begged me to allow her to tell him that I believed it, which I did, for I am convinced it is the case, though at times his actions might have made it difficult to believe. . . . I kissed her when she left."

That Mr. Gladstone was deeply pained by the Queen's behaviour is certain; but his final reference to it in his Diary (January 2, 1896) is as follows: "I place on record . . . my strong desire that after my decease my family shall be most careful to keep in the background all information respecting the personal relations of the Queen and myself during these latter years down to 1894, when they died a natural death. Relations rather sad in themselves, though absolutely unattended with the smallest ruffle on their surface."

Viscount Gladstone took the view that, after the publication of Mr. Buckle's *Life of Disraeli* and the last volumes of *Queen Victoria's Letters*, the Gladstone family were "no longer bound by this inhibition." Into the merits of that delicate, domestic question it is fortunately unnecessary to enter. It must suffice to say that Mr. Herbert (Viscount) Gladstone's *Apologia*, already referred to, appeared in 1928.

The interval craved by Mr. Gladstone between the turmoil of politics and the grave lasted four years. He emerged from his retirement to plead the cause of the Armenian Christians in 1896, but on May 19, 1898, he passed away, and, amid abundant manifestations of public sorrow, was buried in the Abbey.

A full generation has elapsed since Gladstone's death, yet so bitter were the controversies raised by his policy, so hopelessly conflicting the views held of his political conduct, that history still finds it difficult to pass a final judgment on one of the most remarkable careers in English politics. Lord Rosebery, in an eloquent eulogy, insisted that apart from the intense religious convictions which formed "the essence, the savour, the motive power of his life," the outstanding characteristics of the man were "dauntless courage, unflagging industry, a faith which was part of his fibre"—these, he says, "were the levers with which he moved the world." These are qualities which men of all parties and every creed can equally admire. No tributes to his memory were, indeed, finer or truer than those paid in the two Houses by Lord Salisbury and Mr. Balfour—two men, as it happened, who though political antagonists were personal friends. "What he sought," said the former, "were the attainments of great ideals, and whether they were based on sound convictions or not, they could have issued from nothing but the greatest and purest moral aspirations . . . and he will be long remembered . . . as a great example . . . of a great Christian man." "He brought to our debates," said Mr. Balfour, "a genius which compelled attention, he raised in the public estimation the whole level of our proceedings, and they will be most ready to admit the infinite value of his service who realize how much of public prosperity is involved in the maintenance of the worth of public life, and how perilously difficult most democracies apparently feel it to be to avoid the opposite dangers into which so many of them have fallen." Mr. Balfour's words revealed profound political insight in 1898. Subsequent events have given to them an immeasurable and lamentable emphasis. Parliamentary Democracy, as a form of government, reached its zenith in Gladstone's days; he was peculiarly qualified by his endowments to adorn and to commend it. Experience has unhappily proved that, in the sphere of politics, imitation, though flattering, is dangerous. Yet there is nothing in this to detract from the memory of one who, great as an orator and great as a financier, was even greater as a man.

CHAPTER X

THE EARL OF ROSEBERY, THE "MAN OF PROMISE"—UNFULFILLED

THE relations between Queen Victoria and Mr. Gladstone extended throughout a great part of the nineteenth century. Lord Rosebery's aggregate service in Cabinet office amounted to less than half a decade. Yet brief as was his tenure there were among the Prime Ministers of the Victorian era few whose personality was more interesting or more inscrutable. Evidently ambitious, he over and over again declined opportunities which would surely have satisfied any man's ambition. Whether the refusal was due to ultra-fastidiousness, to a morbid self-consciousness, or to genuine humility, it is difficult to know. But the fact remains. He was under forty when he became Foreign Minister, and short of fifty when, after having been Prime Minister, he suddenly retired from the leadership of his Party and ceased to exercise any appreciable influence upon public affairs.

The withdrawal of Mr. Gladstone from the Premiership (March 1894) left his Party in considerable confusion. With a precarious majority in the House of Commons, it had been defeated, on the main item of its legislative programme, in the House of Lords. Nor had Mr. Gladstone left any obvious successor to his place. Of his lieutenants in the House of Commons, Sir William Harcourt was senior in service; if not the ablest he was decidedly the most prominent, and for platform purposes incomparably the most effective. But under no circumstances would

Harcourt have been called upon to succeed. Had Gladstone been consulted as to his successor, he would have suggested Lord Spencer. Mr. Asquith described as "all moonshine" the report ascribed to Harcourt's son that of the Commoners in the Cabinet only Asquith and Mr. Arthur Acland opposed his father's succession. John (Viscount) Morley, who stood next to Harcourt in authority, was definite in his objection to serving under Harcourt, and doubtful whether he could even serve *with* him. But, in fact, the matter was settled entirely by the Queen. She thought it due to Lord Salisbury to intimate to him her intentions, and having done so, exerted all her personal influence (as well as enlisting the help of the Prince of Wales) to induce Rosebery to take office. After stating, according to his wont, his many objections, he eventually agreed to serve. Harcourt consented sulkily, and on conditions (to be noted presently), to serve under him. On March 5, Rosebery kissed hands as Prime Minister, but, despite the Queen's urgent request, refused to retain the Foreign Office, which was given to Lord Kimberley.

Thus at the age of 47 the "man of promise" succeeded to the place vacated by the veteran of 83.

Born in 1847,[1] Rosebery, like his predecessor and his successor, was educated at Eton and Christ Church. At Oxford he made no special mark, and preferring his racing stud to academic honours, left the University prematurely and without taking a degree. At Eton he was considered clever but lazy. "I am doing all I can to make him a scholar," wrote his Eton tutor. "Anyhow, he will be an

[1] Rosebery, fifth Earl of, Archibald Philip Primrose, b. 1847; ed. Eton and Christ Church; Under-Secretary Home Office (1881–3); Lord Privy Seal and First Commissioner of Works in Cabinet (1885); Foreign Secretary (1886 and 1892–4); Chairman of L.C.C. (1889–90 and 1892); Prime Minister and Lord President of Council (1894–5); d. May 21, 1929.

orator, and if not a poet such a man as poets delight in." It was a shrewd forecast. And even more shrewd: "He is one of those who like the palm without the dust."

It was the great misfortune of Rosebery's career that he was not compelled by circumstances to go through more of the dust of life. While still at Oxford he refused a suggestion that he should stand as a Conservative for Darlington. That was sensible; for he had not made up his mind as to his Party affiliations. In 1868, before attaining his majority, he succeeded his grandfather as Earl of Rosebery, and was thus excluded from the chance of sitting in the House of Commons.

It was an irremediable disaster. Rosebery was, with one exception, the only Prime Minister of the reign who never sat in the Lower House. The exception was Lord Aberdeen, and the exception—as so often—proved the rule. Ten years of the rough and tumble of the House of Commons, especially if combined with membership for a popular constituency, might have made a different man of Lord Rosebery. It is not certain; for the defects of his character were congenital. He did, indeed, serve as the first Chairman of the London County Council, having been elected to that body as a representative of the city in 1889; but the Chairmanship, like the Foreign Secretaryship and the Premiership, was virtually laid at his feet. Things came too easily to this spoiled child of fortune, and he treated fortune's gifts just as spoiled children always do. All the same, he did splendid work on the County Council—perhaps (as he himself thought) the best work of his life.

So far from seeking place, preferment, or prominence, Rosebery spent much of his time in finding reasons for avoidance of them. He refused to second the Address in 1868, but consented, under pressure, to perform that not too responsible function in 1871. In 1872 he refused the offer of a Household appointment from Mr. Gladstone, and in 1873 the Lord-Lieutenancy (subsequently accepted) of Linlithgow. His marriage in 1878 to Hannah Rothschild provided him with an adoring wife and great opulence, and in 1879–80 he was Gladstone's host during the Midlothian campaign. That fact furnished a sufficient reason to this sensitive soul for refusing a minor office from his guest in 1880. It may also be that he deemed the Under-Secretaryship for India hardly worthy of his acceptance. In 1881, he did undertake to represent the Home Office, as Under-Secretary, in the House of Lords, but on the understanding that he should have virtual control of Scottish business. His chief was Sir William Harcourt, who agreed with Rosebery in thinking that Scotland ought to have a Secretary of its own. Failing to persuade Mr. Gladstone, who was too busy with Ireland to given attention to Scottish interests, Rosebery resigned in 1883, and went off on a world-tour. His cordial reception in the Colonies laid the foundations of that ardent Imperialism which remained one of the abiding passions of his life. On his return he was admitted to the Cabinet (1884) as First Commissioner of Works, and won golden opinions from Mr. Gladstone, who in 1885 went out of his way to refer to his young colleague as "the man of the future."

But the future in politics was dim. In 1885 the Gladstone Ministry fell, and though Gladstone resumed office in 1886, it was no longer at the head of a united Liberal Party. In the short-lived Ministry of 1886, Lord Rosebery supplanted Lord Granville at the Foreign Office. The Queen categorically refused to entrust the seals of that office again to Lord Granville, or to accept Lord Kimberley in his place. Gladstone was, therefore, obliged reluctantly to acquiesce in the supersession of "his best colleague and friend." Rosebery's appointment gave great satisfaction at

Berlin, not only to the Crown Princess, who wrote to congratulate her mother, but to Bismarck, who "was immensely pleased and hoped and trusted Lord Rosebery would walk in Lord Salisbury's footsteps." He did. Rosebery, overwhelmed by the responsibilities of his position, sought at the Queen's request an interview with Lord Salisbury and showed himself most anxious to maintain continuity of policy in foreign affairs. An acute critic has, indeed, expressed the view that the establishment of the principle of continuity in foreign policy was the most substantial achievement of Rosebery's political career.

His tenure of the Foreign Office lasted, in the first instance, only a few months. From 1886 to 1892 he and his party were in opposition, and it was during this period that he began to draw away from the Manchester School type of Liberalism and attract to himself younger Liberals of a different kidney. "Lord Rosebery," said Lord Haldane, writing of this period in his *Autobiography*, "was one of the most formidable and impressive men in England. . . . His influence on Asquith, Grey and myself was not the less great because he seemed to appreciate fully that Liberalism must, if it were to have a future, be lifted out of the rut into which it was tending to fall. The programme of the future could not be fashioned by the officials of the National Liberal Federation, but only by a statesman with an outlook which was fresh and appreciative of this country as the centre of an Empire. . . . We find in him a pillar of political strength."

Like Disraeli, Rosebery perceived that a new era in world history was dawning; that alike in domestic and in Imperial affairs the day of *laissez-faire* was over. Gladstone remained to the end a convinced individualist; in the social legislation which commended itself to Disraeli, Rosebery, and Chamberlain he was not interested. Still less was he interested in Imperial affairs. If not a little-Englander, he was a little-European. He was gravely concerned about the wrongs of Neapolitans or Irishmen or Balkan Slavs, but much less interested in the rights of our own kith and kin beyond the oceans.

Rosebery thought in continents. Accordingly when Gladstone formed his last Administration (1892), Rosebery was with great difficulty persuaded to return to the Foreign Office. He had lost his devoted wife in 1890; he had become absorbed, thanks to an engagement to write *Pitt*, in literary work; he was increasingly interested in the London County Council, and it needed all the Queen's powers of persuasion, combined with Gladstone's, to drag him back into "servitude." On August 11 Sir Algernon West (Gladstone's secretary) reported that "it was all up with Rosebery, and that he definitely declines, but gives no ground except disinclination for office and politics." He adds in his *Diary*: "The interview between Gladstone and Rosebery was most touching and painful, and they were both nearly in tears." On the 12th the Queen notes that "nothing would induce him"; but on the 13th urges the Prince of Wales to bring his influence to bear. On the 14th the Prince wrote to him from Cowes that he would "deeply deplore" his refusal. "There are," wrote the Prince, "many grave questions at this moment affecting our interests in India, Egypt and Morocco, and it requires a very watchful eye to prevent Russia and France from harming us, and a thorough knowledge of the subject which nobody possesses more than you do. Let me, therefore, implore of you to accept office (if Mr. Gladstone will give you a free hand in foreign affairs, and not bind you to agree with him in *all* his home measures) for the Queen's sake and that of our great Empire." On August 15 Rosebery telegraphed to Gladstone, "So be it." All was well.

Harcourt had from the first been sceptical about Rosebery's reluctance to take office, and when he heard of his declaration that he "was no longer in public life," wrote to Morley: "It is pretty Fanny's way, and we have survived a good deal of it for many years." To Rosebery himself he made the sardonic comment: "Without you it [the new Government] would be ridiculous; with you it is only impossible." Harcourt very soon made it impossible.

Rosebery's own account of the matter is on record. Both to the Prince and to Gladstone he insisted that his difficulty was not "public but private, that his 'long loneliness and sleeplessness had unfitted him for public life.'" In his interview (August 11) with Gladstone he said: "No one not in my skin could conceive the loathing of politics that I had conceived. Gladstone clasped my hand in his and said with the most pathetic violence, 'God Almighty in His infinite mercy and goodness guide you to a right decision,' repeating this two or three times with the greatest solemnity."

Rosebery's reluctance was genuine. Harcourt would have been delighted had he persisted in it. Two years earlier the latter had written to Gladstone: "I fear we are fundamentally at issue with Rosebery on these [foreign policy] questions." Harcourt profoundly mistrusted his "Imperialism," in which he saw, as Lord Crewe writes, "the thing he most detested—Jingoism in a thin disguise." Moreover, he suspected that he was leading some of the younger Liberals, notably Asquith, grievously astray. Leading them he undoubtedly was.

That became increasingly manifest when in 1894, to the bitter chagrin of Harcourt, Rosebery was called to succeed Gladstone as Premier. Rosebery described his seat as "the most uneasy throne in Europe since that of Poland." Within a few months Rosebery and Harcourt were literally not on speaking terms. The latter had consented to remain at the Exchequer and lead the House of Commons only on certain conditions. He was to be free to take independent decisions in the House of Commons without consulting the Prime Minister; to see all the Foreign Office despatches, to have some control of patronage, and to have Cabinets called at his request. No wonder that Rosebery remarked to Asquith that "it might be difficult to serve under Harcourt, but that it would be still more difficult to serve over him."

So it proved. Nor was Harcourt the only lion in the path of the new Prime Minister. The Queen expressed herself as "horrified" at the mention of Disestablishment both for Wales and Scotland in the Queen's Speech. She was deeply concerned also at Rosebery's attitude in regard to the reconstitution of the House of Lords. This was a question in which from the outset of his political career Rosebery had been deeply interested. Harcourt was not interested in it at all. He took a cynical view of the matter, which still prevails in the Party of the left, and expressed it to Morley. "If," he wrote, "you are to have a Second Chamber, you had far better have one which is moderately stupid and tolerably timid, which is what you have got now. . . . I don't believe in 'mending' the House of Lords. . . . There are some things, e.g., the Papacy, which cannot be reformed. They may die, but they will not change."

Lord Rosebery did believe in mending the House of Lords. The Second Chamber problem was one of the most constant preoccupations of his political life. As long ago as 1884 he had moved for the appointment of a Select Committee to consider the best means for promoting the efficiency of the House, and though defeated by 77 to 38 votes, he returned to the attack four years later, and in again moving for a Select Committee laid down certain lines on which reform should proceed. Among these the most important were that the existing Peers, English as well as Scottish and Irish, should delegate their functions to a certain number of representative Peers; that the future Chamber should contain elected Peers and Life Peers as well as Representatives from the Dominions, and that any Peer not sitting in the Second Chamber should be eligible for election to the First.

His motion was again rejected: but the matter was then taken up, half-heartedly, by Lord Salisbury, and by other Peers. In 1907, on the withdrawal of a Bill presented by Lord Newton, a Select Committee was at last appointed to consider the suggestions made for "increasing the efficiency of the House of Lords in matters affecting legislation." The Committee, which sat under Lord Rosebery's chairmanship, presented a most valuable report, advocating drastic changes. Unfortunately the constitutional crisis supervened before legislation framed on the lines of the Rosebery Report could be carried, though Lord Lansdowne did, at the eleventh hour, make an heroic effort to avert, by drastic reform, the revolution involved in the Parliament Bill.[1]

To return to 1894. Lord Rosebery had not been in office many weeks before he forwarded to the Queen (then at Florence) an elaborate memorandum on the question of the House of Lords, and followed it up in the autumn by a speech at Bradford in which he foreshadowed a demand for a "revision of the Constitution."

The Queen, alarmed and indignant, addressed a sharp rebuke to the Prime Minister. Long before this she had evidently come to regret his transference from the Foreign

[1] For details, see Marriott, *Second Chambers* (Clarendon Press, revised edition, 1927), Chaps. XII, XIII, XIV.

Office, "where he was indeed a support to the Queen." It was equally regretted by Rosebery himself, who wrote to the Queen a pathetic account of his difficult position: "He is as Prime Minister more unfortunately situated than any man who ever held that high office. He has inherited from his predecessor a policy, a Cabinet, and a Parliament; besides a party of groups, one of which is aimed against himself. All this is kept in existence by a narrow majority which may at any moment break away. He himself is only able to guide this tumultuous party, through a leader bitterly hostile to himself and ostentatiously indifferent to the fate of the Government. Lord Rosebery in the meantime is shut up in a House almost unanimously opposed to his Ministry, and, for all practical purposes, might as well be in the Tower of London. Under these circumstances, though he hates making speeches anywhere, he has no course open to him but to speak in the country. . . . What then does your Majesty expect of him?"

The Queen sympathized with Rosebery's difficulties, but hoped that he would act "as a check and a drag upon his Cabinet." She added, "speaking very openly to him," a warning that "in his speeches *out* of Parliament he should take a more serious tone and be, if she may say so, less jocular, which is hardly befitting a Prime Minister. Lord Rosebery is so clever that he may be carried away by a sense of humour which is a little dangerous."

To that danger the Queen was not exposed: and on the House of Lords question she was particularly serious. In deep perturbation she wrote to Lord Salisbury for counsel and to ask whether the Unionist Party was "fit for a dissolution now." She also begged the Prince of Wales to try and influence Lord Rosebery, who had "behaved very ill" to her.

Lord Salisbury supported the Queen on every constitutional point she had raised: assured her that the Unionist Party was quite ready for a Dissolution, and added, "though he is very anxious to avoid even the appearance of obtruding his opinions upon your Majesty, it will always be his duty and his pleasure as a former servant of your Majesty, and as a Privy Councillor, to answer any questions which you may think fit to put to him" (October 27, 1894).

The last sentence emphasizes a constitutional point as sound as it is significant. The right of the Sovereign to seek the advice of any Privy Councillor is unquestionable, and it is evidently one which may easily become of high practical importance. The responsible Minister ought perhaps to be informed that the Sovereign proposes to exercise it. If he objects he can, of course, tender his resignation, and the Sovereign will then be confronted with the task of finding a Minister who is willing to accept responsibility. Whether in the present instance Lord Rosebery was informed of the correspondence with Lord Salisbury is not clear: but the point is academic, since Lord Salisbury was evidently prepared to take office if necessary, and so give practical effect to the advice he tendered.

Lord Salisbury allayed, if only partially, the anxiety of the Queen, who constantly recurred to the matter in her correspondence. At the beginning of November (1894) she seriously contemplated demanding a Dissolution of Parliament and an immediate appeal to the country, but before taking so strong a step she decided to consult Sir Henry James and "ascertain his views as to the necessary procedure and also regarding the probable political result of such a step." Sir Henry James, in an elaborate memorandum, minimized the significance of Rosebery's proposed Second Chamber "resolution," which, as he truly observed, could have no practical effect until the proposals for limiting the "veto" of the Lords were embodied in a Bill which could not become law without the consent of the Crown or the House of Lords. To demand a dissolution at once would, he thought, be premature and inadvisable. In that view the Duke of Devonshire and Mr. Chamberlain concurred; but the Queen was still (November 6) "bothered and troubled beyond measure by this House of Lords question." So was Lord Rosebery. He informed the Queen that he was ready, if it would relieve the Queen's anxiety, to resign "to-morrow." But he insisted that he was really the "moderating influence" in his Cabinet, nearly, if not quite, half of which "is in favour of a single chamber. The more prominent people in the Liberal Party appear to be of the same opinion. Lord Rosebery is consequently between two fires." He further assured the Queen that the "Resolution" would "result in nothing. There would be a Dissolution, in which the Government would most likely be beaten," and the Conservatives would come in and reform the House of Lords!

Lord Rosebery's forecast was not immediately fulfilled. His Party preferred the policy of "filling up the cup," that is, of introducing a series of measures which were sure to be rejected by the House of Lords. Opponents applied to the procedure another description, "ploughing the sands." Whichever phrase was the more apt, the policy was ineffective. On June 21, 1895, the Government was defeated in a thin House on a charge of keeping an insufficient reserve of cordite ammunition, and promptly resigned. Their defeat followed immediately upon an important announcement made by Mr. Campbell-Bannerman, as War Secretary, that the Duke of Cambridge, in order to facilitate certain changes in Army administration, was about to retire from the post of Commander-in-Chief. The Duke had filled the post with great satisfaction to the Queen for forty years; he was personally popular with the Army, and it needed all Campbell-Bannerman's tact and firmness to induce him to "place himself in the Queen's hands"—an alternative he preferred to resignation. The Queen wrote "with *much* pain" the necessary letter to her cousin, who, with a tolerably good grace, accepted the inevitable and eventually, though with less grace, consented to withdraw his claim for a pension.

On the day following the announcement of the Duke's resignation Lord Rosebery's Government also resigned. "There had been considerable difference of opinion and Sir William Harcourt had been very disagreeable." So the Prime Minister reported to the Queen. For himself it was "an immense relief." The Queen at once sent for Lord Salisbury. Parliament was dissolved, and the country returned a Unionist majority which remained intact for ten years.

Lord Rosebery's official career was at an end; but he had still thirty-four years of life before him, thus surviving the mistress he had honestly striven to serve, by twenty-eight years. The Queen gave him the Thistle on his retirement, and his last official advice to her was that the Garter should never again be conferred on "non-Christian Sovereigns." "To do so," he added, "is in effect to lower the Garter, to efface its great traditions, and to forget the object of all ancient orders of chivalry."

The relations of Rosebery with the Queen had, throughout his brief Premiership, been decidedly uneasy. Nevertheless, to the Queen, as a woman, he was sincerely attached, and in the Monarchy, as an institution, he had an unshakable belief. His letters to the Queen, especially on unofficial topics, were couched in terms not less courtly than those of Lord Beaconsfield. Those which he addressed to her at the time of the Jubilees of 1887 and 1897, and on the occasion of her drive through the streets of London during the Boer War, though somewhat too obviously composed with a view to publication, are models of their kind, and gave the Queen keen gratification, which she expressed in the first person, so rarely employed. In the letter of 1887 Lord Rosebery wrote of the great procession to the Abbey "with its proud cavalcade of princes, its majestic representation of the sovereignties of the world, and the enthusiastic multitudes that hailed its passage," and then on another note proceeded: "And when later your Majesty passed from the Sovereign to the Mother, the touch of nature which has brought your Majesty into sympathy with the humblest of your subjects added the supreme emotion to a matchless scene. None who beheld that scene can ever forget it; for it was history and human nature blended and compacted in a single glowing picture." Not for nothing had Rosebery studied his Burke and his Macaulay!

Ten years later Rosebery wrote, more briefly and more simply, though not less eloquently, of the celebration of the Diamond Jubilee: "What it must represent to your Majesty of joy and sorrow, of pride and pathos, of the present and the past, I can only dimly guess. To us it has been the splendid expression of a nation's gratitude, the symbol of loyalty, deep, passionate and stedfast, which has encompassed your Majesty's throne, and grown year by year with your Majesty's life, until it has penetrated every remotest corner and subject of the Empire. . . . No capital in the world has ever witnessed such an enthusiasm of devotion to a Sovereign."

More touching still were the words addressed by Rosebery to the Queen on March 15, 1900. Times had changed. The South African War, though the worst was now over, had brought sorrow and humiliation to the subjects of the

Queen; she herself was nearing the end, yet never in her long reign had the Queen been closer to the hearts of her people. Old lady that she was, and increasingly feeble, her courage was dauntless, her energy unimpaired, and she went in and out among her subjects more often and more familiarly than ever before. "I think the visit to London," wrote Lord Rosebery, "far more interesting and touching even than the Jubilees: it was more simple and spontaneous. It was as if a great wave of sympathy and devotion had passed over the capital. . . . Your Majesty does not much admire Queen Elizabeth, but the visit to London was in the Elizabethan spirit. There was, however, this difference, that with the pride that England felt in Elizabeth there was but little love. Now the nation glows with both." Less than a year after these words were written the life and reign of Queen Victoria had ended. The Victorian era, like the Elizabethan era, was part of the historic past.

But we anticipate. To return to 1895. Who, at that time, could have foreseen that Lord Rosebery's official career was closed? But so it was. On August 12 he communicated to Harcourt his "irrevocable decision" not to meet him in council again. To Asquith he wrote on the same day expressing his willingness to stand aside and his opinion that "in our shattered condition" the Liberal Party should not be led by a peer. "But what would be worse," he added, "would be that the Party should be led by a Commons Castor and a peer Pollux who disagree on every subject and communicate on none." In the event, Harcourt remained leader of the Party in the Commons, Kimberley led it in the Lords, Rosebery retained a "titular primacy."

This unsatisfactory and indeed unworkable arrangement could not last. In 1896, as already mentioned, the Armenian massacres brought the old chief out of his retirement.

Rosebery disapproved Gladstone's proposal that England should take independent action in deposing the Sultan. The Party, on the whole, followed Gladstone's lead, and Rosebery finally resigned his shadowy leadership. On October 8 his resignation was publicly announced. His personal relations with Gladstone remained affectionate, but he did not disguise from him the truth that it was he who had "innocently and unconsciously dealt the *coup de grâce* and had precipitated his resignation of a leadership, which he "doubted whether he had ever held." Gladstone was acutely distressed, but the Queen cordially approved Rosebery's conduct.

Rosebery's resignation did not end the troubles of his Party. On December 14, 1896, correspondence between Harcourt and Morley was published in all the papers. Harcourt (as he wrote to Asquith) declared that the situation was "intolerable" and that he had resolved "not to appear in the House of Commons in the approaching session in the capacity of Leader of the Opposition." Sir Henry Campbell-Bannerman was chosen to succeed him. With him, in turn, Rosebery broke in 1902.

Meanwhile, he had given a general support to the foreign and colonial policy of the Salisbury Government, notably on the questions of the Soudan and South Africa. Whatever else Rosebery was, he was an ardent Imperialist. "Imperial Federation," he had declared in 1888, "is the dominant passion of my life." Four years before that he had visited Australia, then in the throes of the agitation against the intrusion of foreign European Powers into the South Pacific. In speeches at Melbourne and Adelaide he gave eloquent utterance to the faith that was already inspiring him. "There is no subject," he said at Melbourne, "so interesting to Englishmen as the future of the British Empire. To many it is merely a fortuitous agglomeration of nations and of countries. To some it is simply a series of accidents. To others it is only a grammatical expression. . . . It is held together by . . . the communion of races. . . . Since my visit to Australia it will become a passion with me to endeavour to preserve that union." At Adelaide he coined a phrase which has become (in Lord Crewe's words) a "commonplace of political terminology." He insisted that Australia had already become a nation, but, "Does this fact of your being a nation," he pertinently asked, "imply separation from the Empire? God forbid! There is no need for any nation, however great, leaving the Empire, because the Empire is a commonwealth of nations." Once more he recited his Imperial creed . . . "I believe that the connection of the British Empire will remain, for the reason that it is desirable for civilization that it should continue to exist."

After his return to England he took part with Mr. W. E. Forster and other prominent men of both Parties in founding the Imperial Federation League. The League did admirable work in arousing public opinion, and to that work Rosebery largely contributed. Rarely was the Imperial topic absent from any of his great speeches. With no little ingenuity he made it the basis of an address to the Trade Union Congress in 1884, and during the next few years he constantly spoke on the subject.

In 1887 a Colonial Conference met in London. It was the first of a series of meetings which have now become an integral part of the constitutional machinery of the Empire. Rosebery presided at a banquet given during the Conference to his cousin, Edward Stanhope, who was responsible for initiating an experiment, destined to increasing success. He took the opportunity to lay down the lines along which the work of the Federation League ought to develop—political connection, defence, communications and commerce. Thanks, in large measure, to his unceasing activity on its behalf, the League gained ground rapidly between the Jubilee of 1887 and that of 1897. Even when at the Foreign Office Rosebery found time to encourage this non-contentious work, and, presiding at the Jubilee banquet of the Royal Colonial Institute in 1893, he reaffirmed his conviction that in periodical Imperial Conferences would be found the solution of "what was called Imperial Federation."

The Jubilee of 1897 marked the zenith of this particular phase of the Imperial movement. The South African War induced a reaction. On that ensued Mr. Chamberlain's Tariff Reform Campaign, which caused great searching of heart among Liberal Imperialists. Lord Rosebery himself was opposed to the project of a *Zollverein*, and the Radical victory in 1906, won largely on the Free Trade issue, damped down Imperialist enthusiasm. Rosebery held that Chamberlain's proposal "would tend to dislocate and in time dissolve the bonds of union of the Empire," and when, in 1907, the time came for a meeting of the Imperial Conference (as it had now become), it met *Consule Asquith*, and in a mood of chastened enthusiasm.

Nevertheless, of the many miscalculations made by German diplomacy, perhaps the most serious was that "the first shot fired in a great European war would be the signal for the dissolution of England's loosely compacted Colonial Empire." The value of the work done by Lord Rosebery and his associates in the Federation League was demonstrated: the Dominions and Colonies, as one man, came into a war, which was recognized as theirs no less than ours.

Meanwhile, Rosebery had been moving farther and farther away from his former colleagues. A great speech which in December 1901 he delivered at Chesterfield

By kind permission of the Proprietors of "Punch"

John Morley — Sir William Harcourt — Sir Henry Fowler — Lord Rosebery — H. H. Asquit

seemed, indeed, to afford some hope of Liberal reunion; it affirmed the desirability of a "clean slate," and urged that the "fly-blown phylacteries of the Liberal Party should be put aside." But, though Campbell-Bannerman was invited to lunch in Berkeley Square, it soon became clear that the rift between Rosebery and his former colleagues had hopelessly widened since 1895. Haldane blurts out the truth in his *Autobiography*: "Rosebery had put himself out of Court"; "he had apparently deliberately rejected the call that came to him after his great speech at Chesterfield." Evidently, there was no room in the same party for ardent Imperialists and "little-Englanders" of the Campbell-Bannerman type. In 1902 Rosebery broke with the latter, and in 1905, on the eve of the election, he made it clear in a great speech at Bodmin that "he would never fight under the banner" unfurled by the Radical leader. The "People's Budget" of 1909 completed the breach. Even his friendship with Asquith, real and deep as it was, could not stand that strain. Rosebery condemned the tactics of the Lords in rejecting the Budget but was opposed to the Parliament Bill of 1911. Yet rather than have the Lords swamped by the creation of 500 Peers, he voted, reluctantly, for the Bill.

The constitutional crisis of 1913 naturally aroused some of his deepest political emotions, but he held that for the Crown to veto the Home Rule Bill would "be unconstitutional and amount to a *coup d'état*." Alternatively he advised that the King should urge his Ministers to call a conference with a view to a compromise between the two Parties. Failing the adoption of that expedient, he suggested that the King should send to the Cabinet a formal minute explaining his position and demand a formal written reply. The Conference met, but ultimately, when almost within sight of success, broke down.

The war ensued. To Rosebery, as to others, the war brought private grief as well as profound public anxiety; his health was failing, but so high did he stand in public estimation, that in December 1916 he was invited to join the Second Coalition Government under Mr. Lloyd George, in a capacity not involving departmental work. He declined the offer, and in the autumn of 1918 was struck down by an illness from which he rallied but never recovered.

The end did not come until 1929: but Rosebery's work was done. For forty years he had been a great figure in the public life of Great Britain and of the Empire. After his retirement from the leadership in 1896 he virtually abandoned party politics, but continued busy both with tongue and pen. As far back as 1890 he had published his brilliant monograph on Pitt, and from the comparative leisure of his retirement he issued in rapid succession three fine studies: *Peel*, *Cromwell*, and *Napoleon, the Last Phase*. A sympathetic sketch of *Lord Randolph Churchill* appeared in 1901; *Chatham, his Early Life and Connections*, in 1910; he wrote an introduction (in French) to Comte Albert Vandal's *L'Avènement de Bonaparte* in 1912, and two volumes of *Miscellanies* were published in 1921.

Of many of Rosebery's great speeches mention has already been made. His type of oratory was better suited to the platform than to the Senate, where oratory is at a discount. Of his speeches in the House of Lords a shrewd critic has remarked: "Lord Rosebery . . . always tended to preach, but ordinarily he showed due respect for his congregation. In the House of Lords he adopted rather the tone of a very consciously sane chaplain addressing the inmates of a home for imbeciles." It is true that he found the atmosphere of the Lords uncongenial, yet he could be at times extraordinarily effective in debate, as, for instance, when he pricked the bubble of the Duke of

Argyll's rather pompous eloquence on the "Gladstonian umbrella."[1] But in general he was less happy in Parliament than outside it. In later years he became generally recognized as the "Public Orator of the Empire," and no one was better equipped for the part; yet the highest perfection of literary eloquence was reached in those more intimate addresses when he was called upon to "appreciate" the life-work of a contemporary or friend. Of such addresses perhaps the palm of excellence should be assigned to his address at Oxford when he unveiled a tablet to the memory of Cecil Rhodes[2] (June 12, 1907).

Yet, in estimating the career of Rosebery as a whole, some words which he wrote about Lord Randolph Churchill come irresistibly to mind: "Randolph appeared a very son of the morning. Nevertheless, because of this very splendour of promise his achievement came infinitely short of anticipation. . . . Such a career, politically speaking, cannot be considered full or triumphant. Why was it not something more?"

The career of Lord Rosebery was not exactly parallel with that of Lord Randolph; yet the resemblance was close enough to suggest that the question put by Lord Rosebery in reference to his friend might pertinently be repeated about his own career, "Why was it not something more?"

[1] House of Lords, *Hansard*, 10 July 1885.
[2] See Marriott: *Oxford* (1933), p. 194.

CHAPTER XI

LORD SALISBURY—THE CLOSE OF AN ERA

AMONG Victorian statesmen Lord Salisbury has a place indisputably his own. The last Prime Minister of the reign, he held the office for a longer period than any of his predecessors. Moreover, if the memory of Bishop Boyd-Carpenter—an intimate friend of Queen Victoria—may be trusted, the Queen regarded Lord Salisbury as the greatest of the long series of her Prime Ministers. Whether her judgment can be sustained is one of the questions to be answered in the following pages. That he was one of the greatest of Foreign Ministers is undeniable; it is less certain that he can be reckoned a great Prime Minister. "A public servant of the Elizabethan type; a fit representative of his great Elizabethan ancestor." Such was the judgment expressed by his immediate predecessor in office. Lord Rosebery's observation was singularly felicitous. He had already, as we have seen, detected something of the Tudor spirit in the mistress; his appreciation of the servant was equally shrewd. Perhaps he had in mind the words addressed by Queen Elizabeth to William Cecil when he took the oath as Secretary:

"This judgment I have of you, that you will not be corrupted with any manner of gifts; and that without respect of any private will you will give me that counsel that you think best; and if you shall know anything necessary to be declared unto me of secrecy, you shall show it to myself only, and assure yourself I will not fail to keep taciturnity therein."

Uncorrupt in more than a material sense Lord Salisbury was; a counsellor who gave to his Queen and his country

By kind permission of the Proprietors of "Punch"

HATFIELD, 1573 AND 1887

THE LORDLY CECIL ENTERTAINS HIS SOVEREIGN

always of his best. He had no "private will" to serve: his sole thought was for the dignity and well-being of his own country, and the peace of the world. Service was his ideal: popularity he not only never sought but positively shunned.

Shy rather than haughty; not too tolerant of society of any kind, and frankly impatient of bores; a scholar and a student; as much of a recluse as a man of affairs can be; happy in his family circle; happier still, perhaps, in the seclusion of his study, protected by double doors, bolted and barred, against all intruders; scrupulous in the performance of his duties as landlord yet somewhat oppressed by his great inheritance; a country gentleman devoid of country tastes; regarding a horse merely as a means of relatively rapid transportation; a devoted servant of the Crown, yet not, like Disraeli and Rosebery, a courtier; a brilliant writer and a finished orator, but without the craving for self-expression and no lover of words; a devout Churchman, but unostentatious in piety, as in other matters of moment; a great English patriot with none of Palmerston's braggadocio; a firm believer in England's imperial destiny, yet devoid of Disraeli's imagination and cautious in encouragement of the imperial idea; lacking in personal magnetism, but nevertheless an acknowledged leader of men; a great party chief under democratic conditions, though a despiser of the arts of the demagogue; by no means devoid of personal ambition yet ready to surrender place and prospects to convictions; singularly free from prejudices but immovable in adherence to principles;—such was the personality of the last of the great statesmen of the Victorian era.

Lord Robert Arthur Talbot Gascoyne-Cecil was born at Hatfield on February 3, 1830.[1] The third son of the second

[1] Salisbury, Robert Arthur Talbot Gascoyne-Cecil, Third Marquis of, b. February 3, 1830; ed. Eton and Christ Church; M.P. for Stamford (1853–68); Viscount Cranborne (1865); Secretary for India (1866–7);

Marquis of Salisbury, he owed much of his intellectual endowment to his mother, daughter and heiress of Mr. Bamber Gascoyne, of Childwell, near Liverpool. Still more he owed to his grandmother, Lady Emily Hill, the daughter of the first Marquis of Downshire. It was these two ladies who, according to a candid descendant, rescued the Cecil family from that "destitution of talent" which for nearly two centuries had distinguished it. From the days of the first Earl of Salisbury—the son of the great Lord Burghley, and himself the wise counsellor of Queen Elizabeth's foolish successor—down to those of the seventh Earl, advanced by Pitt to the Marquisate, "the general mediocrity of intelligence which the family displayed was," in Lady Gwendolen Cecil's words, "only varied by instances of quite exceptional stupidity."

The childhood of the future Prime Minister was solitary and wretched. So bullied at his preparatory school that he could never be induced to send his own sons to a preparatory boarding-school, he fared even worse at Eton. Plainly he was not of the stuff of which popular schoolboys are made. Perhaps something of a prig in boyhood, no good at games, careless in dress, unconciliatory in manner, he was taken away from Eton before he was fifteen.

As an undergraduate he spent two happy years at Christ Church, and made some mark at the Union, but the climate of Oxford suited him so ill that he was advised to avail himself of a nobleman's privilege and curtail his residence by a year.

Marquis of Salisbury (1868); Chancellor of Oxford University (1869–1903); Secretary for India (1874–8); Foreign Secretary (1878–80); Prime Minister and Foreign Secretary (1885–6); Prime Minister (1886–92) and First Lord of the Treasury (1886), and Foreign Secretary (1886–92); Prime Minister (1892–1902) and Foreign Secretary (1892–1900); Lord Warden of the Cinque Ports (1895–1903); Lord Privy Seal (1900–2); d. August 22, 1903.

A younger son, with a meagre allowance, he must needs seek a profession if not a livelihood. Of success in politics, which he placed first in order of usefulness, he was unhopeful; for Holy Orders, which he put second, he deemed himself unfit on grounds of health and—a shrewd bit of self-analysis—his "inaptitude for gaining personal influence"; the Bar he regarded as "a public nuisance"; and so his uncertainty ended in journalism. Meanwhile, he was returned (August 1853), through the good offices of his kinsman, Lord Exeter, as member for the Borough of Stamford.

In 1857, he married, despite his father's opposition, Miss Georgina Alderson, the brilliant daughter of a distinguished judge. Marriage proved the turning-point of his life: it established his health, spurred his ambition, and brought to a solitary, self-mistrustful, and easily depressed man, companionship, assurance and unclouded happiness. From the day of their marriage until death parted them, husband and wife were all in all to each other.

For some years their joint resources were very meagre. Lord Robert had serious thoughts of abandoning politics and seeking a permanent job, but his wife urged him to "play the great game," and he played it: supporting, meanwhile, an increasing family largely by his pen.

Curiously devoid of the desire for self-expression, he took to writing simply as a necessary but distasteful expedient. Yet he owed much to the discipline it imposed and the training it afforded, and was not unmindful of the debt. The literary distinction which characterized his parliamentary oratory was plainly traceable to his apprenticeship to the craft of letters. Whether he was right in his general proposition that excellence in speaking can only be achieved by practice in writing is more doubtful. For seven or eight years he wrote regularly for the *Saturday Review*, at that time the property of his brother-in-law, Mr. Beresford Hope; he wrote some articles for *Bentley's Review*, and after its demise (January 1860) he began to write for the *Quarterly*. Of the thirty-four articles which during the ensuing twenty-three years he contributed to that *Review* a large proportion were on Foreign affairs, the department of politics in which his interest lay.

Thus, in January 1864, he wrote a very remarkable essay on the Schleswig-Holstein question, exhibiting a grip upon the factors of that perplexing problem such as few Englishmen can have possessed at the time, and which not many have since troubled to acquire. He felt acutely the humiliation in which England was involved by the alternations of bravado and cowardice which characterized her diplomacy, and by her failure to redeem her pledge to the small nations which had confided to her their interests.

Of even greater historical, though of less diplomatic significance, was the essay on Poland, published in the previous year (January 1863). Lord Robert's indignation had been deeply stirred in the case of Poland, as in that of the Danish Duchies, by the policy pursued by Lord John Russell and Lord Palmerston.

> "A nation," he wrote, "may uphold its honour without being quixotic, but no reputation can survive a display of the quixotism which falters at the sight of a drawn sword. . . . To threaten or to hint an intervention which you had no earnest intention of carrying out was contemptible as regarded the Power whom you intended to defy, but it was inhuman towards the people with whose agony you were playing."

These biting words expressed a principle to which in later years his own diplomacy very closely adhered.

Except for the brief interlude of Lord Derby's second

Ministry (1858–9) (in which his father was included as Lord President of the Council), Lord Robert was continuously in opposition from 1853 down to 1866. In his daughter's phrase, he was in those days a veritable Ishmaelite; his hand was against every man's, Whig and Tory alike. But by his incisive attacks on the policy of the Government he was rapidly establishing a parliamentary reputation. After 1863 his name appears not infrequently in Lord Palmerston's letters to the Queen, though seldom in a complimentary context. Thus in reference to an attack (misdirected as it happened) on Robert Lowe's conduct at the Education Office, Palmerston wrote (April 18, 1864): "Lord Robert Cecil, who never loses an opportunity of saying or doing an unhandsome thing, lost an opportunity of taking a handsome and generous line, and alone cavilled at and criticized Mr. Lowe's statement." Lord Salisbury did not approve of his son's attitude, particularly towards his own "leaders," and threatened to discontinue the payment of his election expenses. Lord Robert in reply undertook not "needlessly" to attack Disraeli, "much as I dislike and despise the man." Besides, Disraeli's conduct had recently improved. "I trust," added Lord Robert, "that this conduct may continue and that I may never have occasion to mention his name again. But if he recurs to his old courses, I cannot change my convictions to suit his intrigues."

There spoke the man. If his father deprived him of the means to remain in politics, so be it; but with honour he declined to compromise.

In 1865 his elder brother died and Lord Robert became Viscount Cranborne and heir-apparent to his father's title and estates. Thereafter his pecuniary position was assured; but his position in the Party remained ambiguous. In 1866, however, he accepted Cabinet office as Secretary of State for India, serving, of course, under Disraeli as leader of the

House. His first tenure of office lasted only about six months. With his friend Lord Carnarvon and General Peel he resigned rather than be responsible for Disraeli's Reform Bill. In October he contributed to the *Quarterly* an essay on "The Conservative Surrender." That article, one of the most trenchant he ever wrote, revealed his bitterness of soul and his profound dissatisfaction with the working of the Party system. Seven years earlier he had written:

"Party loyalty is good when paid to a worthy object and paid without misgiving. Party discipline is a means to a great end; but in some emergencies and under some leaders it may be made to frustrate the end at which it aims."

To this theme he now returned after his own experience in the Government of 1866–7. He was not unmindful of the conditions which the Party system must necessarily impose upon the conduct of politicians and particularly upon Cabinet Ministers; but he was quick also to apprehend the dangers inherent in it.

"It is," he wrote, "the great end on which all are in common bent which contributes all that is noble or even innocent to party warfare. The tactics of Parliamentary parties are often hardly to be distinguished from faction; the agencies by which they operate upon the wavering or the wayward are often far from exalted: the temptation to purchase allies by concessions of principle is enormous. The one ennobling element, the palliation, if not the atonement, for all shortcomings is that all the members of a party are enlisted in common to serve one unselfish cause, and that it is in that service that their zeal, even when least scrupulous, is working. Take this great end away and parties become nothing but joint-stock companies for the attainment and preservation of place."

His political position was somewhat eased in 1868 when the death of his father gave him a seat in the House of Lords and removed him from immediate contact with his detested leader. Besides, the policy of the Gladstone Government, between 1868 and 1874, gave him ample opportunity for the exercise of his critical faculties. Nor did he neglect it. He declined the leadership of his party in the House of Lords, but from a position of greater freedom and less responsibility he continued instant in criticism of the Radical measures proposed in rapid succession by the Gladstone Ministry. Though strongly opposed to the Irish Church Bill, he advised the House of Lords to pass it on the ground that the measure had received the direct approval of the electorate. To elicit the opinion of the constituencies was in his judgment the primary function of a Second Chamber. When the judgment had, as in this case, been deliberately pronounced, it was not for the House of Lords to persist in opposition.

The Queen's attitude, as we have seen, exactly coincided with that of Lord Salisbury. When the country had pronounced decisively, it was not for the Crown or the Lords to obstruct legislation. Sovereign and statesman had one outstanding quality in common—superb common sense. Both knew when and how long to fight; both knew when and how to give way. That their judgment was never at fault it would be idle to pretend. It would be difficult, for instance, to defend Lord Salisbury's opposition to the Bill for the abolition of University Tests, though it is pertinent to remember that Mr. Gladstone had himself resisted it until he lost his seat for the University. The Bill was opposed by Lord Salisbury not merely as a Churchman and a Conservative, but as Chancellor of the University—an office to which he had been elected on Lord Derby's death in 1869. He greatly prized the honour, but his conception of the duties of the office differed widely from those of Archbishop Laud or Lord Curzon. He disliked "functions," academic or otherwise, as much as Lord Curzon loved them; he rarely visited Oxford, and interfered hardly at all in its internal affairs. He was, however, responsible for the appointment of the Executive Commission of 1877, which carried into effect the principles of the Act of 1871.

The Gladstone Ministry fell in 1874: its fall brought Salisbury face to face with one of the most momentous decisions of his life. Should he accept Disraeli's invitation—not devoid of magnanimity—to join his Ministry, or should he remain, it might well be permanently, in isolation with little power to influence the course of events? To the great advantage of his Party, of the country, and indeed of the world, he decided to accept office and became Secretary of State for India.

This was the real beginning of his official career, and of his intercourse, rarely interrupted, until her death, with the Queen.

Thus far references to Lord Salisbury had reached the Queen's ears from somewhat tainted sources: but when for the first time he stayed at Osborne he made a very favourable impression. "Lord Salisbury (who is particularly agreeable and gentle and who one could not believe could be so severe and sarcastic in debate) . . . dined." Such is the entry in the Queen's *Journal* for January 14, 1875. Subsequent intercourse, increasingly intimate as years went on, confirmed and deepened first impressions. About the Queen's new title in India the Secretary of State was helpful and sympathetic, though characteristically cautious as to the legality of its use in *England*. From November 1876 down to 1878 the Queen was in almost daily correspondence with him about events in the Near East.

That tangled and persistent problem had occupied

Salisbury's mind for many years. His first speech on Foreign affairs dealt with the terms to be offered to Russia for the purpose of ending the Crimean War. Then, as always, he showed himself to be not so much pro-Turkish as anti-Russian. Not less deeply concerned than Gladstone about the position of the Christian subjects of the Sultan, he would gladly have seen the Turks turned out of Europe. But an Indian Secretary had to walk warily in dealing with the Caliph, and could not contemplate with equanimity the prospect of a Russian advance in Asiatic Turkey, still less her "diplomatic invasion" of Persia. About a Russian occupation of Constantinople his views were less decided. Like the Emperor Nicholas I, he was convinced that Turkey was moribund, and in retrospect he clearly regretted that we had in 1853 "put our money on the wrong horse" and had missed a great opportunity for a permanent understanding with Russia based upon a partition of the Ottoman Empire in Europe.

In 1876 Lord Salisbury represented Great Britain at the Constantinople Conference; but all efforts to induce the Turk to carry out a drastic scheme of reform were vain. "Convincing the Turk," he said, "is about as easy a matter as making a donkey canter." What were the Powers to do? On March 23 Lord Beaconsfield reported to the Queen the gist of a discussion in the Cabinet, "the most critical Cabinet of your Majesty's present administration." The Prime Minister insisted on complete unanimity on Near Eastern policy. After the Prime Minister had reviewed the situation in detail, "there was a pause, and then Lord Salisbury spoke: low but clear, and with becoming seriousness. Nothing could be more temperate in tone or manner though he did not avoid the difficulty . . . the religious sentiments of bodies of our countrymen [referring doubtless to Nonconformist support of Gladstone's crusade] could not be disregarded, nor could our own convictions be set aside; still, he was prepared on this vast question to bow to the opinion of the majority of his colleagues, and he had recognized . . . that [it] was in accordance with the views of the Prime Minister." It was: but the Queen's views went far beyond those even of the Prime Minister, and she urged them, with the utmost persistence, upon him, upon Lord Derby and Lord Salisbury. On July 15, 1877, she wrote to the Prime Minister that she felt "so *excessively anxious and* so *seriously* alarmed at the state of affairs," but on the 25th she reported a conversation with Lord Salisbury, "with whose sound views she was greatly satisfied. He is deeply impressed with the importance of our being completely prepared for eventualities. . . . And it is no use putting this off. . . ." The Queen was anxious that the Czar should be categorically informed that England "would *not allow* him to go to Constantinople." Lord Salisbury told the Queen that "this was what he earnestly wished could be conveyed to the Emperor, as he felt sure it would stop him." Little wonder, after this, that the Queen cordially welcomed his succession to Lord Derby, whose hesitations and procrastination had almost reduced her to despair.

Lord Salisbury's first act as Foreign Secretary was to issue (April 2, 1878) the famous "Circular," described by Lord Rosebery as "one of the historic State papers of the English language." Its main purpose was to insist that the Treaty of San Stefano should, *in its entirety*, be submitted to the coming conference at Berlin.

For that conference Salisbury prepared the way by concluding three secret Treaties: one with Russia securing agreement as to the Russo-Turkish boundaries both in Europe and Asia; a second with Austria, binding Austria to support Great Britain's policy at Berlin in return for England's acquiescence in Austria's designs on Bosnia and the Herzegovina; and a third with Turkey providing for an English occupation of Cyprus so long as Russia retained Kars and other recent conquests in Armenia. The Russian agreement was communicated to the *Globe* by the treachery of a clerk in the Foreign Office, and Lord Salisbury was constrained, when challenged in the House of Lords, to deny its authenticity. The ethics of such denials cannot be determined by the canons which govern private intercourse; but the necessity for them, especially when the victim is a man of such unimpeachable honour as Lord Salisbury, is none the less regrettable.

These preliminary conventions smoothed the path at Berlin; when Bismarck misunderstood the modest demeanour of Lord Salisbury, "The old Jew man means business," said Bismarck, "but his colleague is a lath painted to look like iron." The misconception had an unfortunate reaction upon international relations in later years. Lord Salisbury valued his Sovereign's approval of his mission, but was well content that the chief measure of popular applause should be bestowed on his chief. The pomp and circumstance attending on the triumphal return from Berlin were indeed decidedly distasteful to a man who shunned all such demonstrations. A year later Bismarck for the second time[1] sounded England as to an alliance between Germany, Austria and Great Britain. Salisbury was then, as always, against anything like an "alliance," but held that if Austria were attacked by Russia "it would be very difficult for us not to go to her assistance," and wrote to Lord Odo Russell at Berlin that "Germany is clearly cut out to be our ally." "Even our ancient friend Austria," he added, "is not so completely free as Germany from any plans or interests which cross our own for the present" (January 14, 1880).

For the next five years Salisbury was not in a position to

[1] The first was in 1876.

give practical effect to his views. On the death of Lord Beaconsfield (1881) he became leader of the Conservative opposition in the House of Lords, sharing the leadership of the Party, however, with Sir Stafford Northcote. This dual control, despite real friendship between the two men, worked badly, and all the worse by reason of the attacks of Lord Randolph Churchill and his colleagues of the "Fourth Party" upon the authority, rather weakly wielded, of Sir Stafford.

On the fall of Mr. Gladstone's Government the Queen settled the question of leadership by summoning Lord Salisbury.

The composition of the new Ministry was largely determined by the masterful tactics of Lord Randolph. He refused to serve under the leadership of Northcote, and insisted that he should be sent to the House of Lords. Salisbury—to the great satisfaction of the Queen and of all the friends of England abroad—himself took the Foreign Office, Churchill the India Office, while Sir Michael Hicks-Beach became Chancellor of the Exchequer and Leader of the House. Salisbury's first Premiership lasted only 227 days, but it was long enough to enable him to repair, as Foreign Minister, some of the havoc wrought, or permitted, by his amiable predecessor. As the Queen wrote to him (September 1, 1886): "Lord Beaconsfield raised up the position of Great Britain from '74 to '80 in a marvellous manner. Mr. Gladstone and Lord Granville pulled it down again during the five years of their mischievous and fatal misrule, but already in seven months Lord Salisbury raised our position again." This succinct summary, though a trifle crude, was not inaccurate; and it explains the Queen's delight at the return of the Conservatives to power. For by this time they were not merely in office, but had entered upon their long period of power. They were returned in the summer of 1886 on a single issue—the maintenance of the Legislative Union between Great Britain and Ireland. In the preceding winter Mr. Gladstone, as already mentioned, had declared for Irish Home Rule. His apologists maintain that his conversion was hastened by the flirtation between the Conservatives and the Irish Nationalists. Gladstone could see only two alternatives: continued "coercion" or the concession of Home Rule. It was "understood" between Parnell and Churchill that the Conservatives would drop "coercion," and on that "understanding" Parnell promised that the Conservatives should have the Irish vote at the "General Election" (November 1885). The precise nature of the "bargain" may never be disclosed. The fact remains: the Conservatives on taking office dropped "coercion"; whether in November they did in fact receive the Irish vote in English constituencies can never be known. Anyway, in the new Parliament the Liberals numbered 335, the Conservatives 249, the Irish Nationalists 86. Plainly, the Liberals could not hold office without the support of the Irish Party. But the Liberals themselves were not united in favour of Home Rule; on the Second Reading of the Home Rule Bill no fewer than 93 Liberals voted against Gladstone, and brought his Government to the ground. The Bill was defeated by a majority of 30.

On the night of June 7–8, 1886, two hours before the fateful division, Parnell created a great sensation in the House by stating that it was made known to him before the Election that the Conservatives, if they were returned, would pass a measure of Home Rule, and implying that the votes of Irish voters in English constituencies were obtained on the faith of that understanding. "Sir M. H. Beach," as Mr. Gladstone reported to the Queen, "emphatically contradicted the statement of Mr. Parnell. Mr. Parnell then rose and stated positively that he spoke on the authority of one who was then a Minister of the Crown. Challenged to name the individual, he said he would do it when he received permission from him to do it." The individual was the Earl of Carnarvon, who in June 1885, yielding to the urgent request of his old and intimate friend, had accepted the Viceroyalty of Ireland, and, with a seat in the Cabinet, had assumed the chief responsibility for Irish policy.

Whatever may have been the views of his colleagues, Lord Carnarvon at least was convinced that "coercion" provided no permanent solution of the problem, and as early as February 1885 had written to Lord Salisbury that "our best and almost only hope is to come to some fair and reasonable arrangement for Home Rule—with safeguards." Lord Salisbury was "not hopeful," but nevertheless urged his old friend to accept the Viceroyalty, and the latter consented, "knowing that . . . I may implicitly count upon the fullest support of yourself and my colleagues at home." So he wrote to his Chief on June 16; and on July 5 he made a full statement to the House of Lords, announcing that the Government had decided not to renew the Crimes Act, but to adopt a conciliatory policy. On August 1 the famous meeting between Lord Carnarvon and Mr. Parnell took place with great secrecy in an empty house in London. Salisbury was informed beforehand, and received from Carnarvon a verbal and written report of the conversation immediately after the interview. He had, however, on Lord Carnarvon's own admission, "urged me, most properly, to be extremely cautious in all that I might say," and he was dismayed to learn that Lord Ashbourne (the Irish Lord Chancellor) had not been present as a third party at the interview. Lord Carnarvon desired that the Queen, though not the Cabinet, should be informed; but Lord Salisbury demurred. Neither the Cabinet nor the Queen knew anything about the matter. Hicks-Beach, therefore, spoke in perfect good faith.

Two days after the Home Rule division, Lord Carnarvon, named in the Press as the Minister indicated by Parnell, made a statement in the House of Lords. Lord Salisbury would have preferred silence, but finally gave way, only urging that the statement should be "as dry as possible and without any sentiment." Lord Kimberley reported to the Queen: "He [Lord Carnarvon] did not give any information as to the nature of these communications, except that they were made without the cognizance of any of his colleagues, and conveyed no promises. . . ." The Queen would seem to have been annoyed at having been kept in the dark, and Lord Salisbury, writing to her on June 14, 1886, admitted that Carnarvon "acted impulsively and with little foresight," and "took singularly little precaution to protect either himself or his colleagues from misunderstanding." These words, doubtless, represented Salisbury's opinion in June 1886, but he might perhaps have added that Carnarvon's principal colleague was cognizant of the interview, both before and after the event.

The incident has no great significance in relation to Conservative policy in Ireland, which was not deflected either by Lord Randolph's "understanding" with Parnell, nor by Carnarvon's interview. It does, however, throw light on Salisbury's defects as Prime Minister. Not that there was in his Cabinets more friction than usual. Quite otherwise; but Salisbury was essentially a solitary worker. Having never played games, he did not understand the team spirit. He was insensitive to personal magnetism, and did not exercise it. He did his best work in the absolute seclusion of his own study; he arrived, after quiet and concentrated deliberation, at his own conclusions, and liked to carry them out himself. Not that he was an autocrat in the Cabinet.

On the contrary, in matters that did not affect his own Department, he deferred too readily to the opinions of others. Thus, in November 1886, Lord Cranbrook wrote to remonstrate with him: "You must forgive me for saying that you have too much renunciation for a Prime Minister, and that you have rights which you forgo in our deliberations. . . . The position requires your distinct *lead*, and your just self-assertion." Hicks-Beach recorded a similar conclusion:

"Certainly as Prime Minister he did not exercise the control over his colleagues either in or out of the Cabinet that Lord Beaconsfield did. . . . Lord Beaconsfield kept a watchful eye on all his colleagues. . . . Lord Salisbury left them very much to their own devices. . . . I have known Lord Beaconsfield enforce his own view on the Cabinet after all its members but one had expressed a different opinion. Lord Salisbury frequently allowed important matters to be decided by a small majority of votes even against his own opinion."

Lord Carnarvon, too, complained that his chief was too much absorbed in the business of his own Department to give full attention to anything outside of it. The complaint was largely justified. The truth is that Lord Salisbury was intensely interested in the work of the Foreign Office, and rather bored by that which fell to him as Prime Minister. "He hates his office," wrote one of his sons in August 1886, an office, as he himself declared, of "infinite worry, but very little power." Of his own volition he would never have accepted the office, and thrice while holding it he offered to surrender it, once to Lord Iddesleigh and twice to Lord Hartington. In his view a Prime Minister is only the first among equals in carrying out the decisions of the Cabinet. Lord Rosebery concurred, declaring, perhaps regretfully, that the Prime Minister was merely the "influential chairman of an executive jury." But that was not the position of a Gladstone or a Disraeli, still less of a Peel. In an unwritten and flexible constitution like our own everything must necessarily depend on the personality of the Prime Minister. Lord Salisbury was compelled, against his inclinations, to preside periodically at No. 10, Downing Street, but his interest was mainly concentrated on the building opposite.

Mainly, but not, of course, exclusively. From 1886 until his retirement in 1902 Lord Salisbury's *Life* is almost co-extensive with the history of England, of the British Empire, and indeed of the world. Only a few of the many topics on which he was in frequent correspondence with the Queen can here be noticed; and these summarily.

Throughout the whole period of Lord Salisbury's three Premierships home politics were dominated by the Irish question. Not that the record of the Government for domestic reform was barren. Local Government was completely reorganized by the Act establishing elected County Councils (1888); an impulse was given to technical education in 1889, and elementary education was made gratuitous in 1891; Mr. Goschen took advantage of cheap money (1888) to carry through a scheme for the gradual conversion of the National Debt to a 2½ per cent. basis; and in 1897 a useful Act for the payment of compensation in case of accidents to workmen was passed; but the continuous preoccupation of the House of Commons was with Ireland, and with the parliamentary tactics of the Nationalist members at Westminster. With these matters the Prime Minister, being in the Lords, was not primarily concerned. It fell, therefore, to successive leaders in the House of Commons—Lord Randolph Churchill (for a few months only), Mr. W. H. Smith and Mr. A. J. Balfour—to keep the Queen informed on Irish affairs. The Queen was especially emphatic on the necessity for restoring the supremacy of the law in Ireland,—an object which was largely attained by the firm administration of Mr. Balfour as Chief Secretary (1887–91), and by the passing of a *Crimes Act* (1887), which greatly strengthened the hands of the Executive. Nor was remedial legislation neglected. The Land Purchase Act of 1885 was followed in 1891 and 1896 by others on a much larger scale, the cumulative effect of which (with the subsequent Acts of 1903 and 1909) has been to transfer the ownership of the soil of Ireland from the landlords to the tenants. By an Act passed in 1898 Local Government in Ireland was reconstructed, roughly on the lines of the English Acts of 1888 and 1894. That these Acts "solved" the Irish problem cannot, in view of the sequel, be affirmed; but it is undeniable that after twenty years of Unionist administration Ireland was in a more peaceable and a more prosperous condition than it had ever been before.

"Unionist" administration it was. On his return to office in 1895, Lord Salisbury reconstructed his Ministry on lines which have left a permanent impress on English politics. From the moment that Gladstone announced his conversion to Home Rule, Queen Victoria had never relaxed her efforts to induce the Whig leaders to coalesce with the Conservatives. Lord Salisbury, in cordial agreement with the Queen, would gladly, as we saw, have yielded the first place to Lord Hartington in July 1886, but the latter declined. In December the question was reopened. Lord Randolph Churchill, who in July had become Chancellor of the Exchequer and leader of the House of Commons, suddenly resigned, to the amazement of the country and the consternation of his Party. But the consternation was only temporary. Lord Randolph had gravely miscalculated his own importance. His resignation was accepted, and his career was at an end. Lord Hartington again refused office, but with his assent and under urgent pressure from the Queen, Mr. Goschen accepted the Chancellorship of the Exchequer. On the fall of the Rosebery Government in June 1895 the Queen's ardent hopes were at last fulfilled. Lord Salisbury for the third time took office as Prime Minister, but in his Ministry were included the Liberal Unionist leaders, the Duke of Devonshire, Lord Lansdowne, Sir Henry (Lord) James, Mr. Goschen, and Mr. Chamberlain.

Mr. Chamberlain significantly selected the Colonial Office as his own particular sphere of activity and struck the keynote of the administration as a whole. The Queen welcomed his appointment, having greatly changed her opinion of him since 1880. In that year Gladstone had with difficulty induced her to admit him to the Cabinet, though he told the Queen that she would like him "as he was very pleasing and refined in feelings and manner," and had never (like his friend Dilke) "expressed republican views."

Still, during that Government the Queen persisted in regarding him as "the evil genius" of Mr. Gladstone. In 1884 she remonstrated with Gladstone upon the "language of *defiance*" employed by "one whom she has long considered as most dangerous in the Cabinet, and one to whom she fears Mr. Gladstone is inclined to listen far more than to those who hold moderate opinions. His speech, which Mr. Gladstone *should read*, is most dangerous and tending to stir up class against class in a very reckless manner." Gladstone, while protesting that he had "neither time nor eyesight to make himself acquainted with all the speeches of his colleagues," did in fact remonstrate. Mr. Chamberlain, however, repeated the offence, with the result that the Queen bluntly informed her Prime Minister that if he could not restrain his refractory colleague he must dismiss him.

By 1887 the wind was blowing from another quarter. In that year Mr. Chamberlain dined with the Queen; again in 1889 with his "very pretty and young-looking and very ladylike wife," and again in 1894 when the Queen found him "as usual, very agreeable . . . Mrs. Chamberlain looked lovely and was as charming as ever." With the consistent support given by Chamberlain to Unionist policy in Ireland, the Queen was naturally well pleased: but not until 1895 did he join the Unionist Government.

Upon the Colonial Office, where he presided from 1895 to 1903, he left a profound and permanent impress, while his influence upon the general policy of the Government was second only, if it was second, to that of Lord Salisbury himself. Since the latter had taken over the Foreign Office in 1885 the whole world-situation had changed. The old Emperor William was dead, and Bismarck had been dismissed (1890) by the young Kaiser. The persistent aim of Bismarck's policy had been, by sowing seeds of discord between her potential enemies, to prevent the encirclement of Germany. He was extraordinarily successful. By tossing Tunis to France he emphasized the hostility between France and Italy, and brought Italy into the Triple Alliance. By encouraging England to remain in Egypt he prevented any friendship between England and France, and by pushing Russia towards Constantinople and Herat he kept England and Russia apart. But the young Kaiser cut the wires between Berlin and Petersburg. France and Russia drew closer to each other. The relations between France and England, on the contrary, remained so persistently bad, not only in Egypt but in the New Hebrides, in Newfoundland and elsewhere, that in 1887 Lord Salisbury was moved to write to Lord Lyons—no doubt half in jest: "It is very difficult to prevent oneself from wishing for another Franco-German war to put a stop to these incessant vexations."

Did the misbehaviour of France impel Lord Salisbury to embrace Germany? It is difficult to answer that question with certitude. An immense flood of light has, indeed, been thrown upon the diplomacy of this period by the publication of the German documents. Yet much still remains obscure in the relations of England and Germany. On no fewer than six occasions between 1876 and 1903 did Germany approach England with a view to the conclusion of an alliance. On four of them (1879, 1887, 1895, and 1899) Lord Salisbury was in office, but no alliance was concluded. He preferred independence if not isolation. He did go so far as to conclude, in February 1887, an agreement with Austria-Hungary and Italy to maintain the *status quo* in the Orient (including the independence of Turkey), in the Mediterranean, the Adriatic, and the Black Sea. Italy agreed to support England in Egypt, and Great Britain promised to support Italy "at every other point whatsoever of the North African Coast districts, and in particular in Tripolitania and Cyrenaica." This meant, in effect, as an Austrian Professor has pointed out, "the co-operation of the British fleet against French advances in the Western Mediterranean and also against the Russian menace to Constantinople and the Dardanelles." It is, however, erroneous to suggest that in these negotiations the initiative came from Lord Salisbury. On the contrary, from the latter's correspondence with the Queen, it is clear that the proposal came from Italy, that it was strongly supported both from Vienna and Berlin, and that the final result was a "cautiously limited *entente*." A German historian, Professor Oncken, goes so far as to say that "the moral extension of the Triple Alliance across the English Channel" was by these agreements assured. Lord Salisbury, on the contrary, writing to Sir Edward Malet (at Berlin), minimizes their significance. Yet, writing to the Queen

(February 10), Lord Salisbury used significant words: "Short of a pledge upon this subject, it [the agreement with Italy] undoubtedly carries very far the '*relations plus intimes*' which have been urged upon us. It is as close an alliance as the parliamentary character of our institutions will permit." On the difficulties to effective diplomacy presented by those institutions Lord Salisbury frequently insisted. Still more was Parliament a stumbling-block to Bismarck; neither he nor the Emperor William II nor von Bülow ever again touched the high-water mark of "*relations plus intimes*" reached in 1887.

Bismarck fell in 1890, and during the next twenty-four years the diplomacy of Germany pursued a tortuous course. At times the Kaiser showed himself eager to be friendly with England; at other times he was guilty of conduct (as after the Jameson Raid) inconsistent with civility. Yet the rapid advance of Germany in the Colonial field owed much to the goodwill of Great Britain. Previous to 1884 Germany owned not a foot of territory outside Europe. In the course of less than two years (1884–5), she leapt into the position of the third European Power in Africa. She established a Protectorate over Damaraland and Namaqualand, a district with an area of 332,450 square miles, which was afterwards known as German South-West Africa. A second German Colony was established by the annexation of Togoland and the Cameroons. Most important of all, however, alike from the point of view of strategy, of man-power, and of raw materials, was the great province on the east coast with an area of 384,180 square miles and a population of 7,645,770 persons, mostly belonging to strong fighting races. This province became known as German East Africa.

Simultaneous with these German annexations in Africa was the establishment of German possessions in the Pacific.

The northern coast of New Guinea, subsequently known as Kaiser Wilhelm's Land, and the group of islands collectively known as the Bismarck Archipelago, were acquired in 1884.

The German settlements in South Africa and in the Pacific were not, indeed, effected without loud protests from Englishmen on the spot. But to these protests the Government at home refused to listen. "If Germany is to become a great colonizing power, all I say is, God speed her. She becomes our ally and partner in the execution of the great purposes of Providence for the advantage of mankind." So said Mr. Gladstone. Lord Salisbury had no more desire to be "dog-in-the-mangerish" than was Mr. Gladstone. But he was less neglectful of British interests. A Charter granted in 1888 to the British East Africa Company recovered for England that hold over the sources of the Upper Nile which were endangered by Lord Iddesleigh's agreement with Germany in 1886. In 1889 a Charter was granted to the British South Africa Company, and the preposterous claims put forward by Portugal were firmly repudiated, not indeed without friction, but happily without bloodshed.

Agreement with Portugal was followed by agreements with France and Germany. Great Britain recognized the French Protectorate over Madagascar, France recognized the British Protectorate over the islands held by the Sultan of Zanzibar. Germany did the same. She also acknowledged the claims of Great Britain to the northern half of the shores and waters of Lake Victoria Nyanza, to the valley of the Upper Nile, and to the coast of the Indian Ocean about Vitu, and thence northwards to Kismayu. In return, Great Britain recognized German claims to the land north of Lake Nyassa, and ceded to her the island of Heligoland.

This final partition of Africa left France in a territorial sense the largest of African Powers, but much of her territory was desert; Great Britain emerged with an area of something less than 3,000,000 square miles; Germany possessed nearly 1,000,000 square miles. Portugal, Italy, and Belgium also shared in the spoil. It can hardly be necessary to add that though quantitatively inferior to that of France, Great Britain's position, controlling as she did three out of the four great arterial rivers of Africa, possessing in South Africa the only great consolidated area adapted for white colonization, and holding all the most important strategic points on the East, South, and West Coasts, was incomparably the strongest. At the same time, the reasonable claims of other nations were satisfied, and a most difficult and delicate diplomatic corner was turned without a collision involving loss of life. It was a great and a characteristic achievement; for Lord Salisbury was, above all else, a peacemaker. The success that he achieved was not, indeed, dramatic. He would have been greatly dismayed if it had been. He shunned the limelight. He cared nothing for popular applause. Intensely jealous for his country's honour, he was profoundly convinced that her true strength lay in "quietness and confidence." "*Im Herzen ein stolzer Patriot*" was the discerning analysis of his character arrived at by Wolff-Metternich, who as German Ambassador in London had good opportunities for studying it. But patriot though he was, he was no Chauvinist. "Boastfulness or self-congratulation in diplomacy was to him," as a kinsman justly observes, "not only an offence against good manners, but the very way to make the worsted negotiator recognize and resent his defeat." His oft-quoted phrase "splendid isolation" may have been misinterpreted as a description of English diplomacy; but it accurately described his own methods of work. He never went down to the Foreign Office until after luncheon; he employed the minimum of secretarial assistance, and invariably reached his own conclusions before asking his colleagues to endorse them. "His judgment," says his biographer, "worked independently of that of his fellows, and was rarely in complete accord with it; decision was easy to him; fear of responsibility unknown; initiative a normal instinct, and opportunity to translate it into action essential to his content."

Such an opportunity came to him, as we have seen, in 1890, and he redeemed it.

During his later tenure of the Foreign Office (1895–1901) his attention was again concentrated upon the problem of the Near East, and its reaction upon the relations of the Western Powers. The Turks were massacring Armenians; the Greeks in Crete were in revolt against the Turks; in 1897 war broke out between Greece and Turkey; the Greeks were no match for the German-trained Turks, and after a few weeks of war the Great Powers intervened to impose terms of peace upon the combatants.

For Great Britain, however, the real danger-spot, in Salisbury's judgment, was Egypt. From the first he had been anxious to determine the British occupation; partly because he was sensitive about the fulfilment of pledges given by preceding Governments, partly because our presence in Egypt meant an open sore in our relations with France, and above all because it had long cramped his diplomatic style.

"Our position in Egypt . . . is a disastrous inheritance, for it enables the [German] Chancellor to demand rather unreasonable terms as the price, not of his assistance, but of his refusal to join a Coalition against us. . . . He is hard to please. Unless we take the chestnuts out of the hottest part of the fire, he thinks we are shirking our work."

Thus to Sir Edward Malet in February 1887; and to Sir William White in April, "Bismarck is still true to the main principle of his policy—employing his neighbours to pull out each other's teeth." But anxious as Lord Salisbury was that we should "relieve ourselves of an unnecessary burden," evacuation must be contingent upon the fulfilment of responsibilities which we had incurred to the Egyptian people, and the safeguarding of our own Imperial interests.

Closely connected with the problem of Egypt proper was that of the Soudan. After the death of General Gordon at Khartoum the British Government, as we have seen, decided to abandon the Soudan, and for twelve years it remained a prey to anarchy. But by 1896 the Egyptian Army had been completely reorganized by General Grenfell and General Kitchener, and the Government of the Khedive determined to attempt the reconquest of the Soudan. Kitchener was appointed to the command of the Nile expedition, and slowly and patiently advanced towards the completion of his great design. On September 2, 1898, the power of Mahdism was finally annihilated by the great victory of Omdurman. Two days later the British and Egyptian forces were paraded before the ruined palace of Khartoum and the shattered tomb of the Mahdi, and there, on the spot where Gordon had perished, a funeral service was held in solemn memory of the dead knight-errant.

Hardly had Kitchener reached Khartoum when the diplomatic sky became suddenly overcast. The French Government had never forgiven themselves for their withdrawal from Egypt in 1882. For more than a decade they had impeded in every possible way the work of financial and political reconstruction undertaken by Great Britain in Egypt. That task, unwillingly assumed but patiently fulfilled, seemed now to be on the point of final consummation.

Meanwhile, French adventurers had been displaying remarkable activity in Central Africa. The Anglo-German Agreement of 1890 had been followed by a similar attempt to delimit the French and British spheres of influence in the neighbourhood of Lake Chad. In 1894 the British, operating from the east, established a Protectorate over Uganda, and in the same year the French, operating in West Africa, captured the city of Timbuctoo. They also secured from the Congo Free State the recognition of their rights, with certain limitations, to the left bank of the Upper Nile. In March 1895, however, Sir Edward Grey declared that the dispatch of a French expedition to the Upper Nile would be regarded by Great Britain as "an unfriendly act." The situation was, therefore, already delicate when in June 1896 Major Marchand left France to take command of the expeditionary force in the French Congo. In the course of two years and in the face of incredible difficulties this intrepid Frenchman pushed his way from the French Congo across Central Africa, only to find himself, on his arrival at Fashoda, face to face with the British forces.

Kitchener denied Marchand's right to be at Fashoda as the political representative of France; but though the victory of Omdurman was a potent argument, Marchand refused to yield to it. The quarrel was then referred to the diplomatists. Lord Salisbury claimed for the Khedive all the lands over which the Khalifa had borne sway, and made it clear to the French Government that the claim would be asserted by the whole force of Great Britain.

In the autumn of 1898 the two nations were on the brink of war. France, however, gave way, recalled Marchand, and in March 1899 concluded with Great Britain a comprehensive agreement in regard to the Soudan. By this treaty the rights of Great Britain over the whole Nile basin, from the source of that river to its mouth, were acknowledged; France was confirmed in possession of a great West African Empire, but the whole of the Egyptian Soudan was to be subject to the power which ruled at Cairo. Thus the way to the Cape was still open, unblocked by any other European Power. From that moment Anglo-French relations rapidly improved, until in 1904 the Anglo-French Agreement was concluded and France agreed to give Great Britain for thirty years a free hand in Egypt.

Before that Agreement was reached Lord Salisbury was dead. He had survived his Sovereign by two and a half years, but had resigned his offices in July 1902, thirteen months before his death. During the last four years of his official life he had shared power with Mr. Chamberlain, with whose name rather than with Lord Salisbury's the last act of the Victorian drama is associated.

That act was played on an Imperial stage. The setting and significance of the two superb celebrations which in 1887 and 1897 marked the fiftieth and sixtieth anniversaries of the Queen's accession were primarily Imperial. The two Jubilees were indeed made the occasions for the display of affection and loyalty to the person and throne of Queen Victoria such as England had never in her long history witnessed. But they had a wider and deeper significance. As the Queen went in stately procession through the streets of her capital, kings and princes were seen riding in her train; the whole world paid homage to the Queen-Empress. But the unique feature of the celebrations was the presence of statesmen and soldiers from every part of the far-flung Empire. Nor did the Colonial statesmen make the long journey to London merely for ceremonial purposes. They came to initiate a new constitutional experiment—the holding of a Colonial Conference for the discussion of matters of common concern to the Empire as a whole. Since 1887 these Conferences have met periodically. They have always touched cautiously the larger problem of Imperial Federation, but in regard to defence, communications, shipping, and various minor matters, they have rendered incalculable service to the cause of Imperial unity.

That cause derived an immense impulse from Mr. Chamberlain's presence at the Colonial Office, and at the Jubilee celebrations of 1897 enthusiasm reached the zenith. Then came (1899) the outbreak of war in South Africa. It opened disastrously, and, despite the cordial co-operation of the Empire, final victory was long delayed. It was, however, in sight when Queen Victoria died (January 22, 1901).

The Jubilee celebrations had, it seemed, infused new blood into the veins of the ageing monarch. She was profoundly touched by the manifestations of the world's respect and her people's love. When the war broke out she exhibited all her old solicitude for her troops, all her old and unfaltering courage. In the darkest days of the war Mr. Balfour was sent down to Windsor to reassure the Queen in regard to the alarmist reports then current in London. But, as soon as he began his consolatory words, he was at once cut short with that characteristic, quick little bend of the head in which all royalty seemed concentrated: "Please understand that there is no one depressed in this house; we are not interested in the possibilities of defeat; they do not exist." Mr. Balfour returned to his uncle, as we learn from Lady Gwendolen's narrative, enthusiastically appreciative. "It had been splendid to pass from the clamorous croakers in clubs and newspapers into the presence of this little old lady, alone among her women at Windsor, and hear her sweep all their vaticinations into nothingness with a nod."

There was a touch of the same spirit in the Queen's courteous rebuke to the Kaiser when he informed her of his refusal to intervene in the interests of peace between Great Britain and the Boers (March 1900). The British Ambassador at Berlin was instructed, while acknowledging the Emperor's kindness, to inform him "that my whole nation is with me in a fixed determination to see this war through without intervention. The time for, and the terms of peace, must be left to our decision, and my country . . . will resist all interference."

The same spirit impelled her to drive more than once through the streets of London to manifest her sympathy with her people, her anxiety to share their sorrow and their joy. It braced her again for her final effort. In the spring of 1900 she decided, in place of her annual visit to Southern France or Italy, to go to Ireland and so show her appreciation of the gallantry of her Irish soldiers in South Africa. In this decision there was also, it may be, a tinge of self-reproach. "She desired almost passionately (wrote an intimate friend) to be loved by the Irish." Unfortunately she had done little to win their love. Yet it was not withheld. During her three weeks' sojourn she was enthusiastically welcomed by all classes. But the strain involved in this last effort was too great, and, combined with the South African War, undoubtedly hastened the end. On January 22, 1901, in the presence of two sons, three daughters, and her eldest grandson, Queen Victoria passed away.

EPILOGUE

ANY survey, however slight, of the relations between Queen Victoria and her Ministers must suggest certain reflections.

The first is the contrast between the Queen's position and that of her political advisers. Among the latter none exercised supreme responsibility for more than six years at a stretch. The Queen was continuously in power for more than sixty. Her *Letters* and *Journals* prove how seriously she took her duties. The mere reading of the official documents would have taxed any ordinary man's endurance during a brief term of office; the Queen read them regularly for sixty-four years.

Nor was the reading perfunctory. She allowed no detail to escape her. All important points—and some unimportant ones!—were noted at once, and formed the subject of inquiry and correspondence with the Minister concerned. "Superbly," as an intimate wrote of her, "she continued to stand sentry to the business of her Empire"—virtually to the close of her long life. The image is felicitous: never did her vigilance relax: she was on sentry duty to the end.

Unbroken continuity of experience puts anyone at a great advantage. To this is largely due the power of the permanent official in his relations with the parliamentary Minister. A Minister, speaking generally, has hardly time to learn the business of his office before he is out again. The permanent official has all the precedents at his finger-ends. When the official possesses in addition the glamour of royalty, his position is almost unassailable. Moreover, what permanent official has ever rivalled Queen Victoria in length of continuous service? Her knowledge, more particularly of foreign affairs, was immensely helpful to successive Ministers. Nor was it merely book-knowledge, acquired from the perusal of documents. The Queen could bring to the interpretation of documents and the elucidation of policy a personal knowledge of the human factors in the political equation. The family connections of the House of Coburg were extraordinarily wide. In later years Queen Victoria became literally the "Grandmother of Europe," but from the first she had the advantage of being one of a large royal family. Information frequently reached her to which no minister could have had access. She was able to bring influence to bear which no statesman could have exercised. And that influence invariably made for international peace.

The crisis of 1875 is a case in point. Bismarck, deeply chagrined by the rapid recovery of France after the disasters of 1870–1, was eager to renew the war, in order to "bleed France white." Information about his sinister designs reached the Queen from Potsdam. She promptly acted on it; and with the help of the Czar and the goodwill of the German Emperor, Bismarck's little game was stopped.

To pretend that Queen Victoria's judgment was invariably sound would be ridiculous. There were times when, in differing from her Ministers, she was palpably wrong. But in these cases no harm came, for she well understood the constitutional limitations imposed upon her; she knew that in the last resort the opinion of the Minister, backed by Parliament and the constituencies, must prevail. Thus in 1869 she disapproved of the Disestablishment and Disendowment of the Irish Church. But after the appeal to the country she not only offered no opposition herself, but persuaded the House of Lords to acquiesce. Had she been always right, she would not have been human; and human she essentially was. But right or wrong, it was, and is, an immense safeguard that Ministers and Cabinets should be aware that the policy they propose to adopt will have to stand the scrutiny, not merely of a House of Commons, which they can dissolve, but of an experienced, sagacious, and impartial critic who can, in the last resort, appeal from them to the electorate. For the right of Dissolution, as already argued, indisputably belongs to the Sovereign. It is a prerogative not to be lightly exercised; but in reserve it provides an invaluable safeguard.

Emphasis must be laid on the *impartiality* of the critic. Impartiality as between contradictory policies is neither possible nor desirable. But that the Constitution should provide for a critic who is indifferent to party interests, and superior to party claims, is evidently of immense advantage to a polity based on party government. No unprejudiced commentator, surveying the reign of Queen Victoria as a whole, closely scrutinizing her motives as revealed in her intimate *Journals* and *Letters*, can for an instant doubt that her conduct was invariably inspired by one sole consideration. She applied to every proposal submitted to her only one test: did it in her judgment make for the honour and dignity of her country, and the well-being of her people? That she sometimes misinterpreted the reaction to the test is neither here nor there. The point is that the test was invariably applied; that Ministers were aware that it would be, and that they must be prepared to justify the advice they would tender, not by reference to parliamentary exigencies or party considerations, but by that of the national interest.

The modern world would seem to be committed, for better and for worse, to some form of Democracy. Democratic forms may be temporarily set aside by personal dictatorships. Dictatorial rule may be salutary or mischievous, but in neither case is it likely to be permanent. The choice, then, would seem to lie between the type of Democracy evolved in this country—Parliamentary Government under the ægis of hereditary Monarchy—and the Presidential type exemplified in the Constitution of the United States. Both types have their advantages and disadvantages: but this is not the place to set them forth.[1] They have, however, this feature in common: both the British and the American Constitution are native-born; both spring from the soil, and each reflects the political genius of the two branches of the Anglo-Saxon race. At the same time they are severally adapted to widely different conditions. By singular good fortune Englishmen possess a Constitution which has proved adaptable to the government not merely of an insular unitary State, but of a world-Empire. And the keystone of the constitutional arch is the hereditary Monarchy. "You cannot," said General Smuts on a memorable occasion, "make a republic of the British Commonwealth of nations. If you had to elect a President he would have to be a President not only here in these islands, but all over the British Empire —in India and the Dominions—the President who would be really representative of all these peoples; and here you would be facing an absolutely insoluble problem. The theory of the Constitution is that the King is not your King, but the King of all of us, ruling over every part of the whole Commonwealth of nations; and if his place should be taken by anybody else, that somebody will have to be elected under a process which it will pass the wit of man to devise."

These words point to a profoundly significant develop-

[1] I have attempted that task in *The Mechanism of the Modern State.* 2 vols. Oxford, 1927.

ment. That development began under Queen Victoria. The Imperial idea, as now understood throughout the British Empire, was conceived during her reign. It may well be that the historian of the future will point to that conception as the most distinctive and most significant contribution made by the Victorian era to the sum of the ages. Yet shallow critics have asserted that at the end of Queen Victoria's reign "the Crown was weaker than at any other time in English history." Such an assertion implies a complete distortion of perspective. Even in the narrower sense the observation is of doubtful validity. Queen Victoria was, indeed, more truly a "Constitutional" monarch than any of her predecessors. But a "Constitutional Sovereign" is not synonymous with *un roi fainéant*. Despite the evolution of the Cabinet system; despite the responsibility of Ministers and the irresponsibility of the Sovereign; despite the dominance of Party and the rigid non-partisanship of the Crown, there remained to the Crown a sphere of political action which, if wisely left undefined, nevertheless was of incomparable value to the nation as a whole. On this point the testimony of Mr. Gladstone is not merely eloquent and emphatic, but surely conclusive:

"Although the admirable arrangements of the Constitution have now completely shielded the Sovereign from personal responsibility, they have left ample scope for the exercise of a direct and personal influence in the whole work of Government. The amount of that influence must greatly vary according to character, to capacity, to experience in affairs, to tact in the application of a pressure which never is to be carried to extremes, to patience in keeping up the continuity of a multitudinous supervision, and, lastly, to close presence at the seat of Government; for in many of its necessary operations, time is the most essential of all elements and the most scarce. . . . There is not a doubt that the aggregate of direct influence normally exercised by the Sovereign upon the counsels and proceedings of her Ministers is considerable in amount, tends to permanence and solidity of action, and confers much benefit on the country without in the smallest degree relieving the advisers of the Crown from their individual responsibility. . . . The acts, the wishes, the example of the Sovereign in this country are a real power. An immense reverence and a tender affection await upon the person of the one permanent and ever faithful Guardian of the fundamental conditions of the Constitution. She is the symbol of law, she is by law, and setting apart the metaphysics, and the abnormal incidents of revolution, the source of power. Parliaments and Ministers pass, but she abides in lifelong duty; and she is to them as the oak in the forest is to the annual harvest in the field."

Even in the narrower sense, then, it is untrue that the Crown under Queen Victoria was "weak." In the wider sense the assertion is grotesque. The expansion of the British Empire meant the widening of the influence of the British Crown. Under Queen Victoria the Crown became for the first time the centre and symbol of Imperial unity. It supplied the golden link which alone holds together the British Commonwealth of nations. Since the enactment of the *Statute of Westminster*, Parliament has ceased to be "Imperial"; the Crown alone is the guardian and embodiment of such unity as the Empire still retains.

"A little figure in a great age." Such was the sardonic description given by a brilliant historian of Queen Elizabeth. Inapplicable to Queen Elizabeth, it would be still more grotesquely untrue of Queen Victoria. She was, on the contrary, a fit representative of a period, undeniably the most prosperous, and perhaps the greatest, in all English history. With that period her name is accurately and indissolubly associated.

APPENDIX

SHORT LIST OF BOOKS

(Ed.) Esher, Benson and Buckle: *Letters of Queen Victoria.* 9 Vols. (1907–1932.)

(Ed.) Esher: *The Girlhood of Queen Victoria.* 2 Vols. (1912.)

Queen Victoria: *Leaves from her Journal in the Highlands.* (1868.)

—— More Leaves. (1883.)

Sir S. Lee: *Queen Victoria.* (1902.)

Letters from Sarah, Lady Lyttelton, 1797–1870. (1873.)

(Ed.) Sell: *Letters of Princess Alice.* (E. T., 1884.)

Sir T. Martin: *Life of the Prince Consort.* 5 Vols. (1874–1880.)

Duke Ernest of Saxe-Coburg: *Memoirs.* 4 Vols. (E. T., 1888–1890.)

Baron Von Stockmar: *Memoirs.* (E. T., 1892.)

Sir F. Ponsonby: *Letters of Empress Frederick.* (1928.)

L. Strachey: *Queen Victoria.* (1921.)

C. G. Greville: *Memoirs, 1874–1888.*

Torrens: *Memoirs of Lord Melbourne.* (1890.)

(Ed.) Sanders: *Melbourne Papers.* (1889.)

Russell, John, Earl: *Speeches and Despatches.* (1870.)

—— *Recollections and Suggestions.* (1875.)

(Ed.) Lord Stanhope and Cardwell: *Peel Memoirs.* (1856–1857.)

(Ed.) Parker: *Peel Papers.* (1891–1899.)

Duke of Argyll: *Autobiography and Memoirs.* (1906.)

Earl of Selborne: *Memorials, 1896–1898.*

Lord Malmesbury: *Memoirs of an Ex-Minister.* (1884.)

Sir Algernon West: *Recollections.* (1899.)

Lord George Hamilton: *Parliamentary Reminiscences and Reflections.* 2 Vols. (1916–1922.)

Lord Morley of Blackburn: *Recollections.* (1917.)

Lives of Melbourne (Newman; Dunckley); *Russell* (Walpole); *Peel* (Thursfield; Ramsay); *Palmerston* (Dalling and Ashley; Guedalla); *Aberdeen* (Stanhope); *Graham* (Parker); *Derby* (Saintsbury); *Gladstone* (Morley); *Disraeli* (Monypenny and Buckle; Froude; Murray; Maurois); *Cranbrook* (Gathorne-Hardy); *Clarendon* (Maxwell);

Hicks-Beach (Hicks-Beach); *Granville* (Fitzmaurice); *Harcourt* (Gardiner); *Iddesleigh* (Lang); *Churchill* (Churchill); *Rosebery* (Crewe; Raymond); *Salisbury* (Cecil); *Goschen* (Elliot); *Devonshire* (Holland); *Chamberlain* (Garvin).

A FEW GENERAL BOOKS ON THE PERIOD

Dictionary of National Biography.

H. Paul: *Modern England.* 5 Vols. (1906.)
A. Cecil: *British Foreign Secretaries.* (1927.)
G. M. Trevelyan: *British History in Nineteenth Century.* (1922.)
S. Walpole: *History of England Since 1815.* 5 Vols. (1886.)
J. A. R. Marriott: *Mechanism of the Modern State.* 2 Vols. (1927.)
— *England Since Waterloo.* (10th Ed., 1933.)
— *Second Chambers.* (Revised Ed., 1927.)
— *History of Europe 1815–1923.* (1931.)
— *The Eastern Question.* (3rd Ed., 1918.)

INDEX

INDEX